INTEGRATED DISTRIBUTION MANAGEMENT

COMPETING ON CUSTOMER SERVICE, TIME, AND COST

THE IRWIN PROFESSIONAL PUBLISHING/APICS LIBRARY OF INTEGRATED RESOURCE MANAGEMENT

Integration Functions

Managing Information: How Information Systems Impact Organizational Strategy
Gordon B. Davis and Thomas R. Hoffman

Managing Human Resources: Integrating People and Business Strategy   *Lloyd Baird*

Managing for Quality: Integrating Quality and Business Strategy   *V. Daniel Hunt*

World-Class Accounting and Finance   *Carol J. McNair*

Customers and Products

Marketing for the Manufacturer   *J. Paul Peter*

Field Service Management: An Integrated Approach to Increasing Customer Satisfaction
Arthur V. Hill

Effective Product Design and Development: How to Cut Lead Time and Increase Customer
Satisfaction   *Stephen R. Rosenthal*

Logistics

Integrated Production and Inventory Management: Revitalizing the Manufacturing Enterprise
Thomas E. Vollmann, William L. Berry, and D. Clay Whybark

Purchasing: Continued Improvement through Integration   *Joseph Carter*

Integrated Distribution Management: Competing on Customer Service, Time, and Cost
Christopher Gopal and Harold Cypress

Manufacturing Process

Integrative Facilities Management   *John M. Burnham*

Integrated Process Design and Development   *Dan L. Shunk*

Integrative Manufacturing: Transforming the Organization through People, Process, and
Technology   *Scott Flaig*

INTEGRATED DISTRIBUTION MANAGEMENT
COMPETING ON CUSTOMER SERVICE, TIME, AND COST

Christopher Gopal
Austin, Texas
Harold Cypress
San Francisco, California

IRWIN
Professional Publishing
Burr Ridge, Illinois
New York, New York

Sponsoring editor: Jeffrey A. Krames
Project editor: Margaret Haywood
Production manager: Diane Palmer
Designer: Jeanne Rivera
Compositor: BookMakers
Typeface: 11/13 Times Roman
Printer: The Book Press, Inc.

Library of Congress Cataloging-in-Publication Data

Gopal, Christopher.
    Integrated distribution management : competing on customer
service, time, and cost / by Christopher Gopal and Harold Cypress.
        p.   cm. — (The Business One Irwin/APICS library of integrated
resource management)
    Includes bibliographical references and index.
    ISBN 1-55623-578-X
    1. Physical distribution of goods—Management. 2. Business
logistics. I. Cypress, Harold. II. Title. III. Series.
    HF5415.7.G66   1993
    658.7'8—dc20   92–44104

Printed in the United States of America

2 3 4 5 6 7 8 9 0 BP 9 8 7 6 5 4 3

For my wife Diane, whose inspiration and support have gotten me this far.
CG

For my wife Helen, the only inspiration I need.
HC

FOREWORD

Integrated Distribution Management is one book in a series that addresses the most critical issue facing manufacturing companies today: integration. Integration is the identification and solution of problems that cross organizational and company boundaries and, perhaps most important, the continuous search for ways to solve these problems faster and more effectively. The genesis of the series is the commitment to integration made by the American Production and Inventory Control Society (APICS). A few years ago, I attended several brainstorming sessions in which the primary question for discussion was this: What jobs will exist in manufacturing companies in the future—not at the very top of the enterprise and not at the bottom, but in between? The prognostications included these:

- The absolute number of jobs will decrease, as will layers of management. Manufacturing organizations will adopt flatter organizational forms with less emphasis on hierarchy and less distinction between white collars and blue collars.

- Functional "silos" should become obsolete. The classical functions of marketing, manufacturing, engineering, finance, and personnel will be less important in defining work. More people will take on "project" work focused on continuous improvement of one kind or another.

- Fundamental restructuring, meaning much more than financial restructuring, will become a way of life in manufacturing enterprises. The primary focal points will be a new market-driven emphasis on creating value with customers, as well as greatly increased flexibility, a new business-driven attack on global markets—which includes deployment of new information technology—and fundamentally new jobs.

- Work will become much more integrated. The payoffs will be seen through connections across organizational and company boundaries. Included in the trend are customer and vendor partnerships, with an overall focus on improving the value-added chain.

- New measurements that focus on the new strategic directions will be required. Metrics will be developed that incorporate the most important dimensions of the environment. Similar metrics and semantics will be developed to support the new uses of information technology.

- New "people management" approaches will be developed. Teamwork will be critical to organizational success. Human resource management will become less of a "staff" function and more closely integrated with the basic work.

Many of these prognostications are already a reality. APICS has made the commitment to leading the way in all of these change areas. The decision was both courageous and intelligent. There is no future for a professional society not committed to leading-edge education for its members. Based on the society's experience with the Certification in Production and Inventory Management (CPIM) program, the natural thrust of APICS was to develop a new certification program focusing on integration. The result, Certification in Integrative Resource Management (CIRM), is a program composed of 13 building-block areas, which have been combined into four examination modules, as follows:

1. Integration functions.
   Total Quality Management.
   Human resources.
   Finance and accounting.
   Information systems.
2. Customers and products.
   Marketing and sales.
   Field service.
   Product design and development.
3. Manufacturing processes.
   Industrial facilities management.
   Process design and development.
   Manufacturing (production).
4. Logistics.
   Production and inventory control.
   Procurement.
   Distribution.

As can be seen from this topical list, one objective in the CIRM program is to develop educational breadth. Managers increasingly must know the underlying basics in each area of the business; who are the people who work there, what are day-to-day and strategic problems, what is state-of -the-art practice, what are the expected improvement areas, and what is happening with technology. This basic breadth of knowledge is an absolute prerequisite to understanding the potential linkages and joint improvements.

But it is the linkages, relationships, and integration that are even more important. Each CIRM examination devotes approximately 40 percent of the questions to the connections among the 13 building-block areas. In fact, after a candidate has successfully completed the four examination modules, he or she must take a fifth examination (Integrated Enterprise Management), which focuses solely on the interrelationships among all functional areas of an enterprise.

The CIRM program has been the most exciting activity on which I have worked in a professional organization. Increasingly, manufacturing companies face the alternatives of either restructuring proactively to deal with today's competitive realities or just sliding away—giving up market share and industry leadership. Education must play a large role in making the necessary changes. People working in manufacturing companies need to learn many new things and "unlearn" many old ones.

The educational materials available to support CIRM once were very limited. There were textbooks in which basic concepts were covered and bits and pieces that dealt with integration, but there simply was no coordinated set of materials available for this program. Creating these materials has been the job of the CIRM series authors, and it has been my distinct pleasure as series editor to help develop the ideas and facilitate our joint learning. All of us have learned a great deal, and I am delighted with every book in the series.

Thomas E. Vollmann
Series Editor

PREFACE

This book is unique. It treats the topic of integrated distribution from a *business process improvement* perspective.We took this perspective because managers told us they want the best information about how to make a difference in their companies. Most manufacturing companies, and certainly the successful ones, are focusing on business process improvement or innovation in their quest to achieve consistently high customer satisfaction. Integrated distribution management is one of the most important business process areas for these companies. Our experience taught us that a focus on improving those business processes that form the fundamental components of integrated distribution offers ways to strengthen and sustain competitive advantages.

This book, for the first time in a comprehensive way, pairs integrated distribution management with the process improvements needed to reduce cycle time and cost, improve quality, and satisfy customer requirements. This approach places the integrated distribution manager in the forefront of strategic and competitive imperatives facing her or his company.

While most have benefited from a total quality management philosophy—the continuous and incremental improvement approach—leading edge companies also are devoting their energies to *reengineering* their cross-functional business processes. We have seen them achieve dramatic improvements in time, cost, and quality over relatively short times. We have addressed the powerful issues of business process reengineering and continuous process improvement within integrated distribution management and emphasized its integration with the larger cross-functional supply chain context needed for true innovation in integrated distribution.

This book is for progressive and innovative managers. It explains distribution operations within the integrated supply chain and describes the connections to other operational areas (those covered by other texts in the CIRM series). In addition to pioneering a business process improvement approach, the book provides the knowledge of basic customer order management, network design and improvement, inventory management, and business performance measurement that managers seek. As such, we believe that it will provide a valuable reference for those executives who manage integrated distribution, who need to understand its potential corporate contribution, and whose career success depends on satisfying their customers. We have attempted to distill our combined practical field experiences and observations into an easily readable text that can help readers immediately affect their companies' distribution operations. Our book, first and foremost, is a modern practitioner's book.

The text contains several major features. It explicitly describes the process of integrated distribution, its linkages with other operations of the manufacturing company, and the leading edge practices and concepts that we believe differentiate successful companies and offer sustained competitive advantage. It explains integrated distribution processes all companies share and describes the role of information technology in enabling competitive integrated distribution processes. In addition, the text provides a valuable practitioner-oriented bibliography and set of references for the manager.

We wish to thank our wives Diane Rosenberg and Helen Cypress for their support during an arduous process, the editor Tom Vollmann, whose pungent comments and excellent suggestions made this book twice as good as it otherwise would have been, and Jeffrey Krames, our editor, for his support and patience with our pace and mode of operations. We also want to acknowledge the privilege offered us by our valued clients by granting us opportunities to work with them and learn from their challenges.

Christopher Gopal
Harold Cypress

CONTENTS

CHAPTER 1

THE COMPETITIVE ROLE OF INTEGRATED DISTRIBUTION MANAGEMENT

LOGISTICS AND INTEGRATED DISTRIBUTION— THE SCOPE OF THIS TEXT

Logistics (or logistics management) is defined by the Council for Logistics Management as:

> The process of planning, implementing, and controlling the efficient cost-effective flow and storage of raw materials, in-process inventory, finished goods, and related information from point of origin to point of consumption for the purpose of conforming to customer requirements.

The competitive environment facing today's manufacturing firms dictates that "conforming to customer requirements" is not enough. Logistics performance must satisfy, and in many instances exceed, both current and future customer needs to achieve a competitive advantage for the firm. Logistics management includes the integrated management of all activities related to the supply chain to achieve operating objectives at the lowest cost while *proactively* satisfying customer requirements. A good way to introduce the concepts in this book is to define management terms used in this and subsequent chapters. The *integrated supply chain* (or supply chain) is the physical network that begins with the supplier and ends with the customer. It includes aspects of product engineering, procurement, manufacturing, physical distribution, and after-sales service, as well as third-party delivery and supply. The term *logistics management* is often used interchangeably with *supply chain management.*

1

This text, one of a series in the CIRM Series, focuses on *distribution management*, a subset of supply chain management. Distribution management addresses the physical movement and storage of goods, services, and information in the supply chain and includes:

- *Inbound and outbound transportation*—The physical transportation of raw materials, in-process inventory, components, sub-assemblies, and finished goods from supplier to plant, interplant, plant to distribution center, and distribution center to customer.

- *Warehousing management*—The storage and movement of materials within the warehouse and distribution center.

- *Inventory deployment*—The selection of stocking locations, inventory levels at each location, product mix, and management of customer service levels.

While much of the content of the following chapters deals with the management of these issues, the focus of this book is on *integration*—the integration of distribution management along the supply chain and with the rest of the enterprise. As part of a series on integrated resource management, the book covers multifunctional and informational integration of distribution within the enterprise and with other stakeholders. New management methods and techniques are addressed, but details of day-to-day distribution operations have been omitted. The bibliography presented at the end of the book lists several reference texts that, in our view, deal very well with detailed operational issues.

Figure 1.1 depicts the supply chain and the scope of integrated distribution within it. As can be seen, the supply chain spans the planning, value-added, material, and information flow from supplier to customer, while the scope of integrated distribution essentially covers the transportation and warehousing (movement and storage) of all product and the management of finished goods packaging and delivery to the customer.

The following discussions address the movement of material through the supply chain. Material planning, transformation, sourcing, and design—those components of the supply chain other than distribution—are addressed elsewhere in the CIRM series.

FIGURE 1–1
The Supply Chain and Integrated Distribution

Supplier	Sourcing	Inbound logistics	Manufacturing	Outbound logistics	After-sales service	Customers
	Procurement planning Supplier evaluation and management Component engineering	Traffic planning Carrier evaluation and management In-house fleet management Inbound delivery planning and monitoring Raw material/component warehousing	Production planning and scheduling Manufacturing Transportation between plants	Traffic planning Carrier evaluation and management In-house fleet management Outbound delivery planning and monitoring: Plant to DC Inter-DC DC-customer Primary to secondary DC Finished goods Warehousing and warehouse management Inventory planning and deployment	Spares planning and scheduling Service center management Returns/service transportation	

Scope of integrated distribution

3

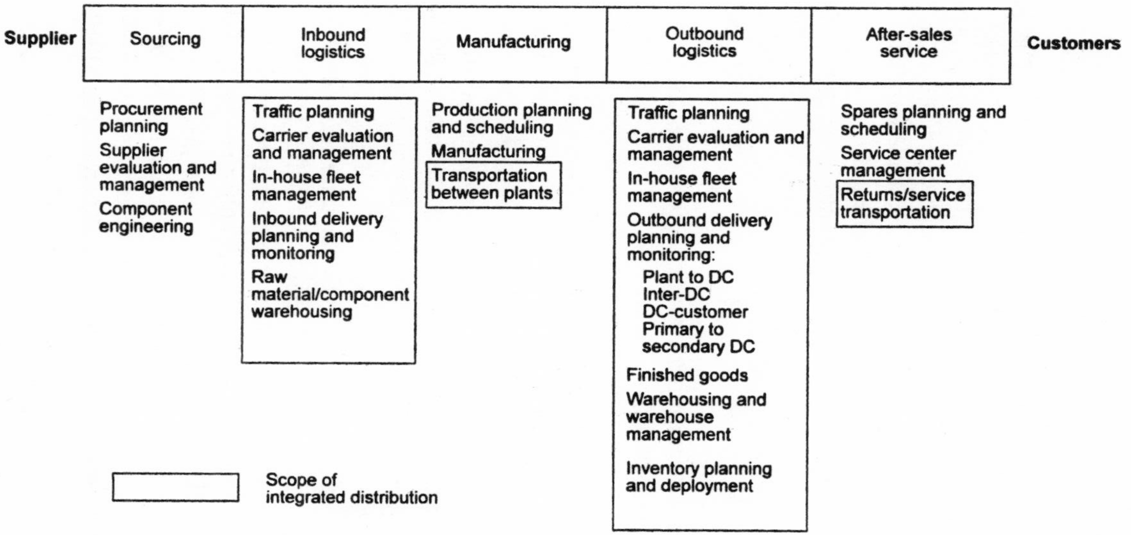

THE STRATEGIC IMPORTANCE OF LOGISTICS AND DISTRIBUTION

The competitive manufacturing environment of today is characterized by a number of driving forces that have compelled companies to change their traditional ways of doing business. In the process, many have had to adopt what amounts to a paradigm shift in their operations philosophy in order to survive. Companies that have not been able to adapt are either extinct or in the process of becoming so. These forces, while familiar to most executives through experience and discussions in the business press, are worth emphasizing here, as they have a significant impact on the distribution function. The major forces and some of their effects on integrated distribution management are explained below.

Shorter and Overlapping Product Life Cycles and Product Proliferation

Increasingly short product life cycles (now measured in months instead of years) and the proliferation of new products and product families are dramatically affecting the management and deployment of inventory in the supply chain to maintain competitive customer service levels. The proliferation of SKUs (stock keeping units) has added a new dimension of complexity to inventory and shelf management, particularly as the products are phased in and out based on marketing strategy and product success.

For example, the life cycle of personal computers (desktops through notebooks and palmtops) has shrunk to months, forcing companies such as Compaq, Dell, and AST to sell multiple and overlapping variations through multiple distribution channels. In the consumer packaged goods field the numbers of SKUs for diapers and soaps have grown exponentially over the past few years. The costs of obsolescence and product nonavailability (not having the right product at the right time at the right place) can be very high in terms of lost sales, lost shelf space, and eroded goodwill. In addition, the risks and competitive costs of poor product introduction, ramp-up and phase-out processes, and inadequate planning and execution in the supply chain have increased significantly. This has forced companies to attempt to integrate distribution with the rest of the enterprise in order to manage delivery based on *velocity through the system* and *availability at time of customer need.*

Increased Customer Service Level and Product Expectations

Customers today, with their expectations set by the best companies across industries, are demanding higher quality at lower cost, rapid response, and immediate availability at the time of procurement and usage. Suppliers are increasingly being measured, evaluated, and certified, not only on the basis of process capability and quality but also on the basis of ability to deliver just-in-time in small lots and at greater frequencies to point of use.

These same suppliers are also being evaluated on their ability to package material for ease of use (for example, semiconductor companies delivering product in cartridges for use on the production line and component suppliers delivering kitted parts in production-ready packaging) and in environmentally safe packaging. Most companies are working to reduce the number of suppliers they use; the suppliers that eventually are selected as part of this trend will be those that have excellent and effective integrated distribution operations.

The service component of the procurement decision is increasing dramatically in importance. Whereas traditional procurement criteria revolved around price and product features, today's buyers are considering such service issues as *delivery, rapid response, quality of delivery and packaging,* and *off-the-shelf availability* as major factors in their buying decisions. These issues now dictate that suppliers manage from the perspective of time-based operations, customer use requirements, and total cost of delivery, rather than short-term transportation, optimum packaging, and warehouse utilization costs.

Advances in Technology

While advances in information and process technologies have often been highlighted as major drivers of business process and change, it must be remembered that they comprise only one component in a series of equally important industry dynamics. Rapid advances in information technology (IT) have enabled the linking of the enterprise to its customers (for example, distribution can receive and process customer orders electronically and in real time) as well as integration of the enterprise itself. Material handling advances, for example, have driven increased automation for quick order turnaround. In addition, the cost of automation now requires packaging designers and operations to reduce such traditional warehousing activities as repackaging, "detrashing" of package materials (collecting, sorting, and reducing used packaging material for recycling or sale as scrap), and re-stocking.

In a broader sense, IT has changed the way the distribution process operates, enabling quick response, increased velocity, and reduction of costs by orders of magnitude. Expert systems have made possible the optimum scheduling of routing, stocking, and delivery, while electronic data interchange (EDI) has changed the basic process of receiving and processing orders and planning for replenishment. Various information technologies have made possible the increasing use of cross-docking and the development of high speed sorters, light-aided order picking, and immediate point-to-point communications in the warehouse. Rapid systems prototyping and advanced development tools and methods have permitted flexibility and the ability to respond rapidly to advances in technologies and changing market needs. Telecommunications advances have enabled instant communication among geographically dispersed operations, allowing *virtual co-location* of inventory source, destination, stocking, and planning points in the supply chain. The virtual office has allowed salespeople to operate independently of a geographic office and to instantly transmit customer requirements and changes downstream in the supply chain.

leading-edge companies have adopted the philosophy of rapid technology introduction and have formalized the IT planning process for distribution to enable them to compete more effectively. Examples of companies that use information technology effectively are Levi Strauss, Wal-Mart, McKesson, Xerox, Milliken, GE Motors, and Dell Computer—all of which have exploited IT along their supply chains and order fulfillment processes to stay ahead of the competition.

Globalization of the Marketplace

Companies are now sourcing, manufacturing, and selling products globally. The global supply chain can span several countries, regulatory and tax environments, customer service expectations, and distribution operating conditions. The importance of distribution as an integral part of the supply chain is emphasized when one considers that logistics costs are greater as a percent of revenue for international firms than for purely domestic companies. Integrated distribution management encompasses international shipping and warehousing as well as inventory deployment and interplant transfers across a number of countries. The increasing complexity of integrated distribution is fueled by operations that encompass multiple cultures, freight forwarders, and management styles.

The Balance of Power between Manufacturers and Distributors

The increase in systemwide capacity in many industries, the shortage of available shelf space, and the concentration and shrinking of available distribution channel outlets has shifted the balance of power toward distributors. This is particularly true for consumer goods companies, including consumer electronics companies (a category that now encompasses personal computers, peripherals, and mobile communications). In addition, the trend toward downsizing of firms and the reduction in supplier company size through restructuring have reduced the bargaining power of manufacturers over an increasingly concentrated distributor industry. This has compelled manufacturers to treat each distribution channel as a major customer in terms of service and delivery needs and to manage for satisfaction of the distributor *and* the customer. This has led to increased trade promotion and spending to move product and obtain increased shelf space, resulting in greater demands in packaging, shipping, and product sales forecasting. An even more significant outcome of this trend is the outsourcing of operations at the supply end of the supply chain—an increasing reliance on distributors to assume many traditional in-house functions, such as procurement, inventory management, and kitting. These dynamics have greatly increased the level of complexity in integrated distribution operations.

Increased Competition and Pressure on Margins

The increasing intensity of competition in virtually every industry has put severe pressure on manufacturers' margins. This has, in turn, resulted in margin and cost pressure being forced back into the supply chain pipeline to upstream suppliers. Within manufacturing firms, this has resulted in increased cost-cutting pressures on distribution with ever-increasing expectations of speed and quality of service. One outcome is close management of cost-customer service level tradeoffs, while another is a shift toward outsourcing of operations that are not core competencies—operations that third parties can perform at lower costs. These third parties include freight forwarders, integrated logistics services firms, contract carriers and warehousers, and external delivery/installation companies.

THE IMPACT ON DISTRIBUTION

The impact of these driving forces on the supply chain and, in particular, the distribution function is significant and has forced manufacturers to compete simultaneously along the dimensions of time, customer service, and cost. These new competitive imperatives include:

- *Improve and maintain customer service* across all dimensions, channels, products, and market segments. These dimensions of customer service include product availability on demand; rapid ad hoc response to customer requests for delivery, information, and order changes; delivery performance to just-in-time requirements and customer request dates; and customization of invoicing.

- *Reduce overall integrated distribution cycle time* from order receipt to delivery/invoicing to hours and days, rather than weeks and months.

- *Increase quality of distribution service,* including order and delivery accuracy, convenience of packaging and lot sizes, and quality and immediacy of response to customer requests for order and inventory status.

- *Reduce total distribution costs* through improved warehousing, inventory deployment, reduced scrap, lower operating costs, and management of transportation costs.

The methods used by leading-edge companies to achieve these distribution imperatives are fast becoming strategic necessities for operational excellence and competitive survival. They span initiatives, focusing on the process and information technology to create what is often called the *virtual enterprise* (an integrated alliance of suppliers, manufacturers, and distributors that appears as a single competitive unit—an operational version of the "hollow corporation") and fall into three categories:

- Business process reengineering, which entails reengineering the integrated supply chain process to achieve quantum improvements in time, cost, and quality *and* the supply-demand planning process to enable quick and flexible response, delivery, and availability of product to competitive customer service levels.

- Implementation of information and automation technologies to manage, plan, and control worldwide supply-demand, resource balancing, and inventory deployment and optimize routing and delivery and deployment to reduce time and turnaround in the warehouse.

• Development of strategic alliances with customers, carriers, and third parties (and, occasionally, even with competitors in different segments of the business) using management methods and information and communications technologies. In the process, several traditionally in-house activities are likely to be outsourced.

Distribution is a crucial component of the service-marketing mix. A truism that is increasingly accepted in industry is that while marketing is a demand-creating activity, distribution is a demand-satisfying activity.

Integrated distribution excellence results in strong customer relationships, and the imperatives described above often represent the criteria for excellence used by customers to evaluate suppliers.

Conversely, excellent distribution can increase customers' switching costs and help build barriers to entry, thereby contributing to a sustainable competitive advantage. This dynamic has been realized by leading firms, which have responded by transforming distribution from a stock-and-ship-it function to a major point of customer contact and an important part of the supply chain. A major reason behind many recent mergers has been the strategy to acquire or consolidate distribution for multiple products, channels, and geographics and therefore increase economies and/or market coverage.

This strategy serves to augment product offerings to the customer, permits consumer product companies to go national with essentially regional brands, reduce *total* distribution costs as a percentage of sales volume, and, in the final analysis, obtain stronger bargaining power over the trade.

The list of companies that have used integrated distribution and the supply chain for competitive advantage is long and impressive. It includes Baxter Healthcare, Abbott, General Electric, McKesson, Dell Computer, and Procter & Gamble (in their relationship with Wal-Mart addressing electronic communications, replenishment, and shipment methods). Some of the ways in which these and other forward-thinking companies have done so include:

• Locating warehouses near customer sites to enable rapid response. This results in customer-specific stocking and trades off increased facility costs, inventory carrying costs, and potentially, transportation costs to achieve quick response. A major electronics OEM company located a warehouse next to a major customer's plant, despite projections of increased overall network costs. This resulted in a high level of customer switching costs and increased customer dependency—crucial in this time of increasing competition among peripherals manufacturers.

- Linking their inventory systems with those of their largest customers to facilitate planning and quick response. A leading semiconductor firm ties its systems directly to those of its distributors, giving them access to inventory figures and the ability to place orders directly, thereby improving *their* response to customer demands.

- Utilizing EDI in accepting and responding to customer orders and specifications. A major apparel/textile company accomplishes 75% of its customer interactions through EDI, ensuring the ability to communicate rapidly with their customers, respond quickly to customer demands for product, and reduce their overall processing costs. In several instances, this required the manufacturer to bear some of its customers' investment costs in the new technologies.

- Automating warehouses and material handling/movement to assure rapid order turnaround—utilizing the knowledgeable worker to an increasingly greater extent in distribution. A large number of manufacturers have installed automated storage/retrieval systems (AS/RS) to automate their warehouses. One equipment manufacturer encouraged and recently required its employees to obtain external education (including APICS certification) in technology, concepts, and management methods.

- Developing integrated information systems and implementing technologies that plan for material along the supply chain, from supplier to customer. Several firms, for example, are in the process of designing and implementing global information sharing systems (utilizing information warehouses and communications technologies) to link the entire supply chain. Baxter Healthcare's ValueLink and Levi Strauss's order replenishment system are prime examples.

- Outsourcing areas and functions not within their core competencies, including contract warehouses and carriers. Xerox, for example, uses third-party carriers for product delivery, removal, and installation. Some companies have outsourced their entire outbound distribution operations to turnkey logistics firms—in effect, entrusting this set of activities to suppliers that make it their core competency.

- Using customer-specific packaging in production line and OEM-ready lots. Several semiconductor firms supply chips in cartridges that are production-ready for shop floor assembly/insertion equipment, and many consumer goods companies ship in packaging ready for shelf display. In the same vein, many computer peripherals manufacturers ship their OEM products in customer-specific packaging that can be sent directly to a customer or dealer without intermediate handling.

- Taking on functions such as inventory management, procurement, kitting, stocking, and delivery directly to the work cell, which are not within their customers' core competencies and turning them into value-added services—making them their own core competencies. One major electronics equipment manufacturer on the West Coast has its entire floor stock inventory, including component testing, managed by a distributor. On the other side of the supply chain, several electronics distributors have set up value-added activities to supply pre-assembled and tested subassemblies and, occasionally, major subsystems to their customers. This effectively reduces their customers' production, testing, planning, procurement, and order processing costs and allows them to focus on *their* core competencies.

- Viewing distribution as a part of the entire order fulfillment cycle instead of merely a function, hence undertaking speed and cost reduction efforts in an integrated customer-oriented fashion instead of striving for functional simplification and localized cost-cutting. Companies such as Xerox, Apple Computer, Intel, and Georgia-Pacific, for example, explicitly recognize this through their focus on the integrated supply chain. All these companies have forced, or are attempting to force, supply chain integration through a consolidation of authority and/or oversight. Over the past few years, an increasingly large number have established vice president/executive level logistics positions. As a result, the integrated supply chain has been explicitly elevated as a major enterprise process.

ACHIEVING IMPROVEMENT AND CHANGE

The vehicles used to implement these changes and achieve the often radical improvements required involve the adoption of new management methods and cultures and span the improvement spectrum, from incremental to dramatic. They include:

- *Continuous process improvement*—the philosophy, culture, empowerments, and techniques of total quality management. This is an incremental and continuous approach to improvement that focuses on subprocesses.

- *Business process redesign (or business process reengineering or business process innovation*—the terms are often used interchangeably)—the total redesign of major cross-functional business processes from the ground up (a "blank sheet of paper" approach). Processes are defined as a combination of process flows, information technology, people, and the organization, using information technology, employee empowerment, and self-managed work teams as key enablers of the redesigned process. Business process reengineering is dramatic in terms of change and scope and provides significant improvements in time, cost, and quality.

These methods and philosophies—one incremental and the other dramatic—their concepts, methods, and implementation issues, are covered elsewhere in the CIRM series. They, however, represent significant improvements in management and operational effectiveness and long term results over typical cost reduction efforts, which tend to focus almost exclusively on personnel and spot cost reductions across the board.

Figure 1.2 shows the relationships between continuous process improvement, business process redesign, and cost reduction efforts. Continuous process improvement and business process redesign are entirely compatible philosophically and in their appropriateness to today's competitive environment (continuous process improvement is necessary for maintaining and improving on the results and platform provided by business process redesign) and, indeed, are necessary if supply chain operations are to be turned into a competitive force.

FIGURE 1–2
Improving Distribution Performance: Continuous Process Improvement and Business Process Redesign

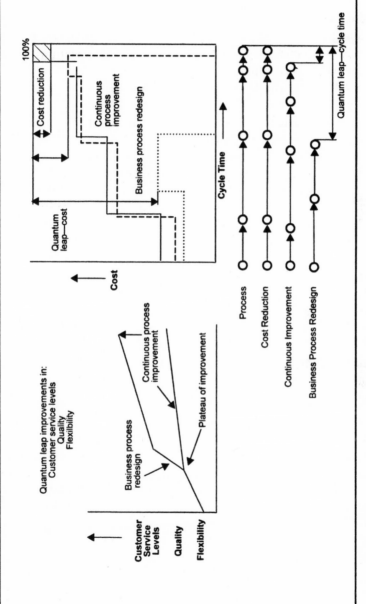

INTEGRATED DISTRIBUTION

These strategies and efforts involve a departure from the traditional ways of doing business—a shift in the paradigm of distribution management. Traditionally, companies have organized, managed, and measured themselves and their performance along fairly narrow functional lines. In such corporations, the charter of distribution typically was to reduce transportation and warehousing costs and provide safe storage and quick order turnaround. Related functions—material planning and scheduling, procurement, manufacturing, and customer service—typically operated in isolation from one another and from distribution management. These functional "silos" optimized narrow interests while de-emphasizing the performance of the enterprise relative to customer and business results. Functional performance measures, often in conflict with one another and the corporate goals, only served to exacerbate the situation.

The concept of logistics management—the integrated supply chain— provides the multifunctional, enterprise perspective necessary to delight customers at the lowest total cost. We cannot adequately discuss integrated distribution management without placing it within the context of enterprisewide logistics management. The new paradigm of logistics management includes distribution as an integral part of the supply chain.

While this text specifically addresses the concepts, issues, and linkages of distribution management, it is presented as an integral part of the overall supply chain and enterprise, hence the term *integrated distribution management*. The remainder of this text will address:

- The overall logistics strategy planning framework, providing a perspective of distribution planning within the framework of the supply chain.
- The management and measurement of distribution operations— warehousing, transportation, and inventory management—and their integration within the supply chain.
- Information technology requirements for integrated distribution.
- Advanced concepts used by leading-edge firms and a paradigm of the logistics enterprise that drives them.
- The linkages of integrated distribution with the supply chain and the enterprise.

LESSONS FOR MANAGERS

The integrated supply chain constitutes one of the primary cross-functional processes (or mega-processes) of the manufacturing company, the others being customer contact-to-cash collections and product concept-to-manufacturing. As such, its effectiveness in supplying product to the customer at the right time, place, and quantity and at the lowest total cost is crucial to the firm's success. Distribution is a major component of the integrated supply chain. It is imperative that managers view distribution as an integrated part of the supply chain, rather than as a series of traditional stand-alone functions—traffic, warehousing, and finished goods inventory management. The theme of this book and the CIRM series is integration—integration within the supply chain and the enterprise. Distribution managers must view distribution as part of the entire order fulfillment cycle. Efforts to increase speed and reduce costs must, therefore, be cross-functional and involve managers from other areas of the organization; integrated distribution affects and is affected by other functions. Localized efforts can compromise companywide initiatives and goals while optimizing subprocesses.

The overriding lesson for distribution managers is that change, and a great deal of it, will be an ongoing feature of the corporate environment. The changing industry dynamics of radically shorter product life cycles, increasing product and option proliferation, higher service level expectations by customers, and rapid advances in information and process technologies and their use by competitors have all come together with structural changes such as globalization of the marketplace and the shift in the balance of power from manufacturers to distributors to create a tremendous increase in competition and pressure on margins. These changes are forcing companies to reevaluate their perspectives on distribution and look for innovative ways of improving the process and using distribution as a competitive weapon.

Distribution managers must be prepared to deal with change on a daily basis and be able to drive and support the tools and techniques being used by leading companies to achieve such change. These tools include continuous process improvement and business process reengineering. While continuous process improvement can achieve incremental levels of improvement in subprocesses and functional processes, it cannot provide the overall dramatic levels often required to stay ahead of the competition. To achieve such significant improvements, leading companies are increasingly looking to business process reengineering—the redesign of major cross-functional business processes from the ground up, using information technology, employee empowerment, and self-managed work teams as key enablers of the redesigned process.

It must be borne in mind that process reengineering, while providing huge competitive benefits in terms of cost, time, quality, and service, frequently requires significant investments in resources, information technology, and training and can entail major organizational changes. The effort must be driven from the very top of the organization and will involve the integrated supply chain. Distribution managers must be prepared to play a significant role in initiating and implementing change. Business process reengineering, by necessity, forges the integration of the supply chain and the rest of the enterprise. It involves procurement, manufacturing planning, finance, after-sales service, information systems, marketing, and sales. These components are all part of, or support, the supply chain and distribution management.

This chapter presents several concepts that distribution managers can use to improve effectiveness and increase customer satisfaction. They generally revolve around *linking with customers* through distribution operations (locating warehouses near customer sites to enable rapid response, for example) and information technology (methods include using EDI and linking inventory and ordering systems with those of major customers to facilitate planning and quick response) and *outsourcing* functions that do not fall within their core competencies (contract warehousing and carriers, for example). On the revenue-enhancing side of the equation, linking with customers includes providing value-added services—in effect, assuming in-house functions traditionally performed by customers. Examples include providing packaging and delivery in production line and OEM-ready lots and providing services such as inventory management, procurement, kitting, stocking, and delivery directly to the work area. Linking with customers through operations, information technology, and value-added services increases customer dependence and provides a true competitive alliance.

CHAPTER 2

LOGISTICS STRATEGY AND DISTRIBUTION ALIGNMENT

Distribution management, a core component of the logistics or supply chain, is an integral part of a firm's logistics strategy. Hence, it forms a significant part of the logistics strategy planning process, with distribution policy aligned with the firm's overall logistics strategy. Logistics, the movement of material and information across the supply chain, is one of the three main management areas in an enterprise. The other two are manufacturing (transformation) and marketing (selling). The logistics strategy, therefore, must be consistent with the corporate goals and strategy of the organization and must be developed in conjunction with, rather than as an adjunct to, the manufacturing and marketing strategies.

LOGISTICS STRATEGY—THE CONTEXT FOR DISTRIBUTION OPERATIONS

Figure 2.1 shows a logistics strategy planning framework that links manufacturing, marketing, and logistics.

The thing that links logistics, manufacturing, and marketing—the glue that binds the enterprise together—is information technology. Traditionally, these elements were loosely linked by information flows (some structured, some ad hoc) across functional silos. Today's competitive environment demands immediate and accurate information sharing across an integrated supply chain. While marketing strategy is externally oriented and manufacturing strategy is internally oriented, logistics strategy provides the interface between the internal and external environments. It consists of five interrelated components:

FIGURE 2–1
Logistics Strategy Planning Framework

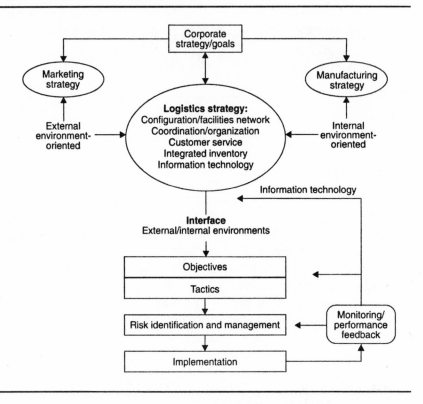

- *Configuration/facilities network strategy*—The network (location, size, mission) of manufacturing facilities, distribution centers, and service centers that provides cost-effective, competitive market coverage.

- *Coordination/organization strategy*—The management and organization structure, control mechanisms, and methods that allow the firm to plan for and manage the logistics network effectively.

- *Customer service strategy*—Customer service levels for the various products, market segments, and geographies that provide customer delight without unnecessary excellence and at competitive costs.

• *Integrated inventory strategy*—Inventory deployment and replenishment across the supply chain, which allows the firm to meet planned customer service levels, market planning (product introduction, ramp-up, and phase-out), and cost objectives.

• *Information technology strategy*—The planning for, acquisition of, and implementation of information technology and systems that enable the logistics business processes and provide a competitive edge in terms of customer bonding, employee empowerment, and immediate global information sharing. The key information technology areas in integrated distribution include warehousing management systems, financial systems, transportation and route management systems, EDI, distribution requirements planning, decision support tools and optimization models, and field service systems.

Supporting these five logistics strategy components is transportation policy and practice, the physical link between supply and delivery points in the supply chain.

LOGISTICS STRATEGY DEVELOPMENT—KEY ELEMENTS AND DISTRIBUTION MANAGEMENT DRIVERS

It is important to understand the scope of logistics strategy prior to discussing distribution management and its integration within the enterprise. Distribution is composed of a series of tactical elements in logistics and should be discussed within its overall context. This section provides this overall context and discusses a framework for logistics strategy. Briefly, an approach to logistics strategy planning is shown in Figure 2.2. The steps are described below.

THE LOGISTICS MISSION

Companies develop coherent logistics missions consistent with their corporate, marketing, and manufacturing strategies. The mission of logistics provides the overall supply chain charter of the firm, forms the basis for its key success criteria, and has important implications for the firm's customer contact operations. Its formulation and execution significantly influence the firm's competitive ability; the absence of a coherent logistics strategy can

FIGURE 2–2
Approach to Logistics Strategy Planning

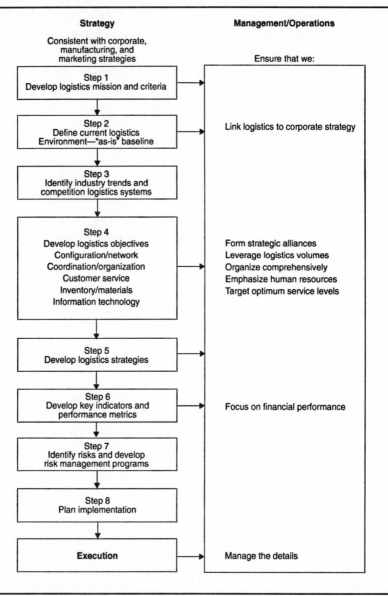

Source: Christopher Gopal and Gerry Cahill. *Logistics in Manufacturing*. Homewood, IL: Richard D. Irwin, Inc., 1992.

place the firm in the position of reacting to the marketplace and its competitors, lacking clear direction for the future. The mission statement cannot, therefore, be a vague collection of "motherhood" statements. It must be thought out carefully, because it will become the firm's operating credo, positioning the firm relative to the market and its competitors. The mission must provide a *vision of excellence and competitiveness; align the logistics, manufacturing, and marketing strategies;* and *encompass the integration of the supply chain.* The mission sets the tone and direction for the distribution operation and its integration with the supply chain.

DEFINITION OF THE CURRENT LOGISTICS ENVIRONMENT—A BASELINE

For many firms, the definition of the current logistics environment often provides the first detailed examination of overall logistics operations. The logistics environment must be defined with hard data, including:

- *Product/material groups and volumes* at each stage of the supply chain.
- *Network source-destination links and flows*—the movement of material and information through the supply chain.
- *Customer service levels and inventory deployment*—along all dimensions of customer service, some of which include delivery performance, backorders, lead time response, order and delivery accuracy, order cycle times, and return and repairs cycles. Inventory deployment must identify inventory levels by product/material at various stages and take into account safety stocks, obsolescence, and stockout risks.
- *Total cost by stage* to address all cost elements—direct and indirect personnel (the latter including attributable corporate and headquarters support, MIS, and finance), inventory carrying costs (at true rates, which can range from 18% to 50% of the unit cost per year), and operational costs such as manufacturing, warehousing and packaging, transportation by mode and type (overnight or next day air, for example), order processing, subcontracting, and field service.

• *Asset utilization*, including in-house fleets, warehousing, field service centers, distribution centers, and manufacturing plants.
• *Information systems and technology* environment, including platforms, connectivity, and problems with usage and implementation.

This baseline is also vital in assessing current distribution operations to identify improvement and waste elimination opportunities. It provides the as-is model against which the future to-be logistics environment will be compared, and it is a core process step in both continuous improvement and business process reengineering methods. The managers of one company discovered that their order turnaround time in the warehouse was not (as they believed and planned for) 48 hours for all products but, rather, for only certain product categories (about 60% of the total). This was because these products were specifically staged and handled; order turnaround could take as long as seven days for other products. This led to customer dissatisfaction, because the company promoted 48-hour turnaround across the board. The baseline thus highlighted a significant opportunity for improvement, and a quality team was formed to focus on achieving 48-hour turnaround for all products. This goal was attained for 95% of all orders within a four-month time frame.

INDUSTRY TRENDS AND COMPETITIVE ADVANTAGE

Another role of integrated distribution management is in the identification of industry trends and competitors' logistics systems to avoid "wasted excellence" and gain a competitive advantage. The firm must know what its competition is doing and what level of service its customers are willing to pay for. The danger in setting absolute targets for levels of customer service without ascertaining customer needs is that the cost of service increases exponentially for incrementally higher levels of service.

At some point it ceases to become cost-effective, unless the customer is willing to pay for increased service or it is felt that the projected service can provide an undeniably sustained competitive advantage through a "quantum leap" in performance. If very high service levels are defined by the competition and form customer expectations, then they become a competitive necessity. However, as Figure 2.3 illustrates, there is a danger in achieving levels of excellence that are not required by the marketplace.

FIGURE 2–3
Meeting/Exceeding Customer Expectations for Service

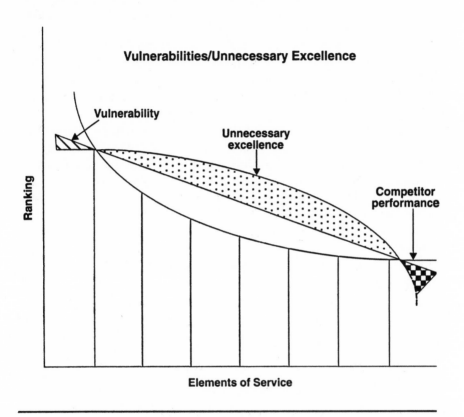

To be cost-effective, the firm must pick and choose its areas of competitive excellence so that it either *exceeds customer expectations* or *beats competitor performance*. Absent one of those conditions, unnecessary excellence typically means wasted money.

On the other hand, such excellence along certain dimensions can provide a competitive marketing opportunity, and shortfalls in service can help identify areas where improvement and rapid action are needed. One major consumer electronics company developed an order turnaround system that would replenish dealer stock within 24 hours. On reviewing customers' needs and the service offered by competitors, however, the company discovered that this turnaround exceeded expectations and was not necessary to ensure customer satisfaction in a majority of instances. By increasing their promised turnaround to 48 to 72 hours as a standard and maintaining the 24-hour response for only a few customers, the company realized considerable cost savings through transportation consolidation. Most orders could be shipped in full truckloads rather than in less-than-truckload (LTL) shipments as had been done almost exclusively in the past.

Another electronics company believed it had obtained an advantage by responding to orders more quickly than its competition. On further analysis, management found that this was not the case. A key issue with their customers (distributors) was the turnaround of after-sales service products sent back to the manufacturer's plant for repair, an area in which this company's response was comparatively poor, taking anywhere from two to five weeks, much longer than a key competitor required for similar service. This information allowed them to focus their efforts on improved spares stocking, setting up a separate line for repair, and an information system that allowed distributors to check the status of repair orders so they could respond to customers' inquiries.

DEVELOPMENT OF DETAILED LOGISTICS/ DISTRIBUTION OBJECTIVES

A firm must develop objectives for its logistics and distribution operations. These objectives must be based on corporate objectives (typically standard operating objectives because they are quantifiable and enterprisewide) and the logistics mission statement. Logistics objectives should be developmental (direction-setting) and must involve line management in their formulation. In order to be useful, they must be direct, concise, and measurable. From these higher level logistics (or supply chain) objectives, a set of detailed distribution objectives can be developed. This cascading set of distribution objectives serves to integrate distribution operations with the enterprise direction and provides measures for monitoring and execution. The measures ensure consistency and accountability and must be process-

FIGURE 2–4
Some Examples of Objectives Related to Distribution

Supply Chain

> Return on operating assets: 15%
> System-wide inventory turns: 10

Integrated Distribution

> Deliver 95% of orders 100% complete within one day of customer request date.
>
> Offer delivery of completed orders within a one-week cycle time from receipt of order.
>
> Offer major customers 48-hour response with complete orders to their emergency requirements.
>
> Ensure, through packaging, that customers receive undamaged product 100% of the time.
>
> Minimize inventory investment while providing stated customer service-level goals*: inventory goal to be consistent with corporate inventory turns goal.
>
> Enable the linking of suppliers and customers for improved service, with EDI linkages accounting for a minimum of 60% of order-requirement communications.
>
> Enable a single point of customer contact by 1996.
>
> Leverage corporatewide and systemwide traffic activities to obtain the lowest possible transportation costs and obtain the best possible service from our contractors: Objective is a 5% reduction from last year.
>
> Manage traffic to support stated customer service level objectives.*

* Customer service goals as defined separately by product-segment.

and customer-focused. They must revolve around the basic performance metrics of cost, cycle time, quality, and customer response. An example of objectives relating to distribution in one firm is shown in Figure 2.4.

ADDRESSING LOGISTICS STRATEGY ISSUES

Logistic strategies must be geared toward rapid customer response and changing market conditions and must be flexible and robust. An executable strategy should involve the smallest combination of risk and capital expenditure in a phased manner and must be integrated with risk identification and risk management programs (contingency planning). The five major categories of risk include business risk, competitive risk, market risk, implementation risk, and operational risk. Risk management programs must provide rapid recovery capabilities in terms of technology, process, facilities, production and inventory deployment, and people. This is the key to the development of a robust strategy, one that enables quick response to changing conditions. It allows the firm to avoid anarchy in its operations should the internal or external environment suddenly change.

Finally, an important element of logistics strategy is its justification for capital and other expenditures. Because of the historical perspective of operations as a "black box" and the finance-driven nature of many companies, justification has typically involved arbitrary hurdle rates. This has resulted in a lack of investment in strategic projects with longer term returns. Hence, logistics strategy investments must be justified using both economic and strategic analysis. This is usually more a cultural change than a policy one.

COMPONENTS OF LOGISTICS STRATEGY

The primary components of logistics strategy—configuration/network, co-ordination/organization, customer service, integrated inventory, information technology, and transportation—must be addressed explicitly. All of these and their major distribution issues are briefly discussed below.

Configuration/Network

The four primary drivers of configuration strategy are process staging, time/proximity, market preferences, and total network cost, each of which must be examined in light of the firm's competitive posture.

Process Staging
Process staging is the coupling or decoupling of a firm's core transformation activities. This includes deciding whether to build a product line completely in one location (e.g., all power tools in the Wisconsin plant) or divide the process among several locations (semiconductor fabrication in Singapore, assembly in Taiwan, and test in California). In addition, it involves such

decisions as whether to build a single large plant or several smaller plants (e.g., building the same line of workstations both in California and on the East Coast). Of equal importance are the issues involving the location of distribution facilities around the world—market coverage and inventory deployment. In many companies, this decision has evolved over time, generally after the initial plant and distribution center locations have been chosen. Primary considerations include process technologies, product technologies, information technology, and the key business success factors.

Distribution Impacts. Every network combination involves trade-offs in transportation, operating, and investment costs; inventory levels; and customer service. These trade-offs are shown in Figure 2.5. Essentially, the greater the number of facilities, the greater the cost in systemwide inventory. A greater number of distribution centers increases market coverage and service levels—at the cost of inventory and transportation. Similarly, an increase in market coverage and service level results (usually) in an increase in sales along with an overall increase in costs. This is the distribution manager's challenge—to maximize market coverage and service level at competitively low overall cost levels. An additional planning factor involves postponement strategies—the points at which products are earmarked for a particular customer. Each type of postponement strategy—labeling, packaging, assembly, manufacturing/fabrication, and time—has its own associated costs, including inventory carrying, warehousing, processing (labeling, packaging, assembly, manufacturing), transportation, and lost sales. These costs must be identified and the strategies evaluated against the benefits of quicker order fulfillment and decreased manufacturing line complexity.

Time/Proximity
The processes within a company that determine the configuration of the logistics network involve proximity and time. These are interrelated, as geographical proximity often determines the elapsed time for major processes and time determines competitive success or failure. Figure 2.6 outlines the time/proximity dependencies of several of the key business issues, the functions involved, and the impacts of these dependencies on distribution. As can be seen in Figure 2.6, the greater the dispersion of the supply chain and the engineering and manufacturing functions, the greater the risk of poor performance along several dimensions, due primarily to information

FIGURE 2–5
Relationships and Trade-Offs

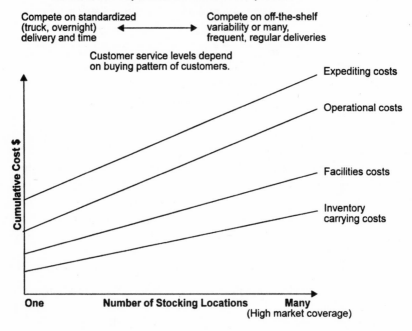

Total Costs, Inventory, and Number of Stocking Locations

The trade-offs depend on the bases of competition.

Compete on standardized (truck, overnight) delivery and time ←————→ Compete on off-the-shelf variability or many, frequent, regular deliveries

Customer service levels depend on buying pattern of customers.

Expediting costs

Operational costs

Facilities costs

Inventory carrying costs

Cumulative Cost $

One   Number of Stocking Locations   Many
                                                (High market coverage)

sharing complexity and increased transportation and inventory costs. Information technology, however, enables the virtual co-location of many of these functions, facilities, and processes through shared information, groupware, and communications networks. Re-engineering of the cross-functional business processes involved, focusing on the integration of process flow, information technology, and organization, provides an ideal vehicle by which to achieve virtuality and overcome time/proximity constraints.

FIGURE 2-6

Key Factors, Their Functions and Geographical Dependencies

Key Business Issues	Functions Involved		Dependencies and Impact on Distribution
Engineering change management	Engineering ←——→	Manufacturing	Greater distance increases complexity and leads to delays, errors, and miscommunication.
Concept to market New product introduction Configuration introduction and management	Engineering ←——→	Manufacturing Supplier Third party	Lower degrees of co-location result in delays of product introduction and incorporation into the supply chain. It also results in poor delivery accuracy where multiple sources are involved.
Response to customer demands	Manufacturing Distribution Field service ←——→	Customer	Greater distances result in increased in-transit inventory and longer cycle times in responding to customer demands—particularly short lead time and ad hoc demands. Also increases risk of transit damage.
Planning response inventory stocking	Supply-demand ←——→ Planning	Manufacturing Distribution Supplier/stages	Increased dispersion leads to planning complexity and information lags, resulting in higher stockouts and safety stocks.
Information flow	Facility 1... ←——→ Corporate	Facility 2,3... Supplier Customers	High degree of network dispersion can result in greater risk of information lag and communication translation, impacting all aspects of distribution.
Total supply chain cost	Supplier Manufacturing Distribution ←——→ Customer	Supplier Manufacturing Distribution Customer	Greater distances can result in increased transportation costs, inventory levels, cost of damage and stockouts. Multiple facilities also tend to duplicate common operating and facilities costs.

Distribution Impacts. Essentially, the more dispersed the network, the more difficult it is to plan, coordinate, and execute to a high level of response to customer demands and product availability. It is here that the effective use of information technology proves powerful, enabling the *virtual co-location* of the network. Developing and implementing a quick response network (including those most neglected aspects—forecasting and safety stock planning) becomes a competitive necessity.

Market Preferences

Market preferences are the customer and market requirements that must be satisfied or exceeded before a firm can succeed in business. They include specific customer delivery preferences (JIT, unitization, production and stock-ready packaging, etc.), order preferences (delivery patterns, level of response), location of major customers and customer segments, regional demand patterns and modes (that differ from national patterns), and country- and region-specific customer expectations. Conforming to and exploiting distribution market preferences are fast becoming key differentiating factors. One large foods manufacturer maintains full-service warehouses regionally and stocks, packs, and ships to the preferences of its regional customers. By doing so, it effectively competes with regional brands and is far more successful than its national competitors.

Distribution Impacts. A major challenge for the distribution manager is to manage for individual customer response in terms of shipment modes (containers, doubles, small trucks), master packaging, routing, and response to ad hoc emergency demands. Centralized planning and carrier selection is, therefore, not an acceptable answer in many situations. One major manufacturer selects and mandates its carriers nationally to obtain a low cost structure. However, at the regional and district level, sales managers often use small local carriers (and, sometimes, large nonapproved ones) for many types of delivery, based on their response to local market preferences. Some large customers demand certain types of packaging, shipment, and delivery (one large manufacturer, for example, requires production-ready packaging in manufacturing lot sizes in set sequences, delivered every 12 hours at the dock). The distribution function that meets these requirements has obtained a significant advantage over its competitors and, in the process, has raised the switching costs of its customer.

Total Network Cost

Managing for total network cost implies evaluating the costs incurred from supplier to customer (and after-sales service) as a single cost structure, with the explicit understanding that no one piece can be improved without affecting the rest of the supply chain. It is the optimization of the supply chain cost structure against trade-offs in customer service levels.

Distribution Impacts. It is imperative that an accurate costing system (preferably an activity-based costing system) be maintained to provide a true cost picture. Any major cost reduction efforts in transportation (consolidation of shipments, for example) or warehousing must be undertaken from the total cost perspective. Consolidation, for example, while providing cost savings in transportation, may jeopardize overall response to customer demands.

Coordination/Organization Strategy

Coordination is defined as the "linking of like activities along the value chain," while the *organization structure* defines the roles, responsibilities, and culture necessary to manage the supply chain effectively.

According to the research of Bowersox and others, the advanced competitive logistics organizations have several common key organization characteristics that include flexibility and the use of process-based performance measures and monitoring mechanisms. They are leaders in the use and innovative development of information technology for decision support and management to integrate the supply chain and the information needs of the company. Many of these advanced companies view outsourcing, partnerships, and third-party alliances from a strategic perspective based on core competencies, cost, flexibility, and customer service and use these approaches in developing a virtual supply chain organization with a formal integrated management structure and process. As part of their management processes, many of them utilize costing systems that provide real-time profiles of true product costs by segments, links, and key success indicators and incorporate strategic logistics planning within the formal business planning process.

Most companies adopt these characteristics through a progression along a continuum, using several interrelated approaches in the process. These approaches include:

- Coordinating (through performance measurement or policy) logistics activities, including marketing, sales, procurement, manufacturing planning, inventory planning and deployment, distribution, and customer support, to develop a process focused on the customer.

- Developing an organization that moves away from the traditional functional organization toward one that provides single-point authority over the supply chain and the order fulfillment process.

- Implementing a culture of continuous process improvement, in which the focus is on the incremental improvement of the process and the culture of continuous improvement. This topic is addressed elsewhere in the CIRM series, notably in the texts on quality and strategic manufacturing. Today, companies are increasingly using business process redesign of major cross-functional processes to obtain improvements in performance (cost, quality, and time).

Distribution Impacts

Historically, distribution has operated within a functional silo, receiving product from manufacturing and third parties, often in an unplanned or unexpected fashion. The new logistics organizations place the distribution function under a broader supply chain umbrella, while newer supply-demand planning systems (distribution requirements planning, while not exactly new, is a good example) force the planning integration of the supply chain. Distribution managers can increasingly expect to see decisions made that are nonoptimal for their functions but geared toward the supply chain goal of providing excellent customer service. These, however, must be accompanied by measurements that monitor performance based on supply chain, not functional, performance—yesterday's measures in today's environment are a sure recipe for disaster.

Customer Service Strategy

Effective customer-focused service strategies start with the philosophy of continuous improvement and one of its basic tenets—internal/external customer orientation. Every employee has a customer, and the enterprise is viewed as a supplier-customer chain, with the external customer being the final point of satisfaction. Developing customer service strategies involves measurement of the company's performance relative to its competitors and the needs of the market, adopting best practices, and analyzing the total cost-service trade-offs. Service forms an increasingly large part of the customer buying criteria; product superiority is no longer enough. Customer service is measurable, and the measures for distribution include:

- Order fill rate.
- Order accuracy and completeness.
- On-time delivery performance.
- Order response cycle time.
- Response to emergency customer requirements.
- Damaged goods.
- Presence (inventory stocking distance to customer).
- In-stock inventory levels/availability.
- Customer access to inventory/order status.
- Response to customer complaints.
- Packaging convenience.

Setting profitable customer service strategies involves analyzing the trade-offs between true total costs and customer service (see Figure 2.7). Some of the primary cost factors involved are material, packaging, marketing/sales, overhead and indirect costs, costs of transportation and warehousing/distribution center operations, inventory carrying costs, and costs associated with after-sales service. Increased incremental customer service levels typically result in increased sales (through increases in goodwill, convenience, and product availability and pre- and post-sales service) but at exponentially rising costs. Optimum service levels, therefore, balance increased sales revenues with the cost increases associated with incrementally higher service levels. Optimum service levels are achieved at the point of greatest overall margin—not at the greatest sales level or the lowest cost. It is obvious that these margins can vary with product lines, distribution channels, and costs of selling.

Most of these costs are distribution-related. True and total costs must, therefore, be known if the company is to optimize its customer service levels. These are the costs that are actually expended and can be measured; there are, however, significant intangible costs, such as goodwill, that must be estimated through customer contact. A key message is that costs increase exponentially with a marginal increase in service levels after a certain point.

FIGURE 2–7
Logistics Management Cost Trade-Offs

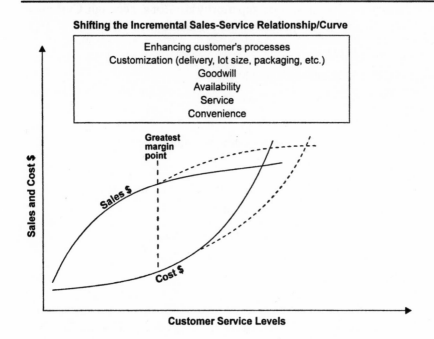

Shifting the Incremental Sales-Service Relationship/Curve

Enhancing customer's processes
Customization (delivery, lot size, packaging, etc.)
Goodwill
Availability
Service
Convenience

Greatest margin point

Sales $

Cost $

Sales and Cost $

Customer Service Levels

Shifting the Cost-Service Level Relationship/Curve	Costs
Business process reengineering Customer contact to cash Supply-demand planning Integrated supply chain management	Operations costs Administration/overhead Information technology costs
Logisitics network rationalization Inventory deployment Traffic reorganization	Inventory carrying costs Facilities costs Transportation costs

In a similar fashion, major cost increases will result in sales increasing in a diminishing manner after a certain point.

An additional element in customer service strategy is after-sales service. Many companies are moving toward alliances and outsourcing of field service based on customer account fragmentation, product mix, and margin to provide the best after-sales service to their customers at the most desirable cost and profit structure.

In setting customer service strategies, a distinction must be made between the customer and the consumer or end customer. For most companies, their actual customer is the retailer, distributor, or wholesaler—the channel of distribution. Strategies must be developed to satisfy both—the customer at the end of the supply chain and the consumer. Among the strategies typically used to manage channels are education of the channel's sales and support force, sales force assistance and initiatives, incentives for stocking inventory and pushing sales, inventory on consignment, and alliances.

Distribution Impacts

Achieving the right cost-service level balance is the challenge of integrated distribution. Reducing costs dramatically (through an arbitrarily corporate-mandated cost reduction goal, for example) may adversely affect service levels and, ultimately, sales. On the other hand, it must be realized that increasing customer service levels will, inevitably, require an increase in investments. Analyzing these cost-service level trade-offs requires the evaluation of the cost structure *along the supply chain* and involves a number of different analytical methods.

Figure 2.8 identifies the areas that must be analyzed in making these cost-service trade-off decisions. It illustrates the fact that the supply chain contains several cost categories and areas that must be considered. For example, inventory costs ($I1$, $I2$, $I3$, $I4$) include WIP, semifinished product (that can be sold as is or further processed), finished goods, packaging and spares, and inventory that resides at customer sites or is under consignment. Transportation costs (T) subsume all transportation expenses, including interplant and inbound transportation. Facilities costs (F) must be carefully considered to account for owned versus leased versus contract facilities (including third-party facilities costs), while operating costs should include activity-based costs of material movement and handling, storage, order processing, and shipment processing (including the cost of expediting).

Finally, the cost of information technology, a key cost area that is often ignored, must be included. Analyzing the supply chain, therefore, is a complex task that requires good cost and operational data.

Figure 2.9 illustrates the various methods that are used for analyses under different conditions. These conditions for analysis range from local analysis (setting safety stocks in a particular regional distribution center, for example) to systemwide analysis (optimization analysis of the entire supply chain to determine optimum inventory deployment or network configuration at the lowest total cost, for example). Whereas local analysis techniques are useful for setting policy at particular points (as in setting safety stocks, the decisions will change frequently over time depending on market demands, product introductions and phase outs, and market coverage strategy), the more global techniques are useful for developing strategy and longer term tactics through what-if analyses. For instance, one firm varies market coverage and anticipated regional demand to determine strategies for distribution center location or contracting.

Analysis methods that fall within this spectrum include financial modeling. In its simplest form, this can be spreadsheet analysis that alters cost relationships based on different cost, transportation, and inventory level assumptions. More sophisticated financial modeling uses specially designed software packages (such as IFPS) that can vary assumptions and incorporate logic into the analysis and analyze enterprisewide cost structures—analyses that would be extremely unwieldy with simple spreadsheets. One should bear in mind, however, that the methods of analysis are contingent on the scope and conditions of the situation being analyzed. The customer service strategies for moving product through retailer shelves described above impose a different set of demands on distribution, ensuring that stocking levels and delivery can support marketing promotions and the attendant demand peaks.

Integrated Inventory Strategy

Inventory deployment strategies are key in maintaining customer satisfaction and have profound effects on the integrated distribution operation. Inventory is, in effect, the buffer between the supply chain and the customer. The just-in-time philosophy indicates that inventory is evil. In these days of increasing customer expectations, however, inventory deployment and safety stock management are necessary and viable strategies for maintaining high

FIGURE 2-8   Making Major Trade-Offs—Areas for Analysis

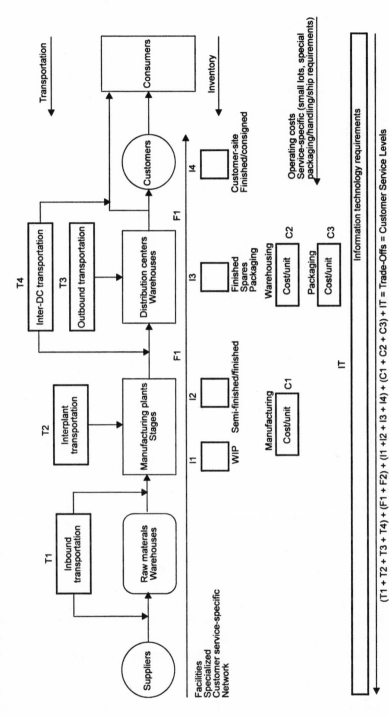

Source: Christopher Gopal and Gerry Cahill. *Logistics in Manufacturing.* Homewood, IL: Richard D. Irwin, Inc., 1992.

FIGURE 2–9
Making Cost Trade-Offs—Methods for Analysis

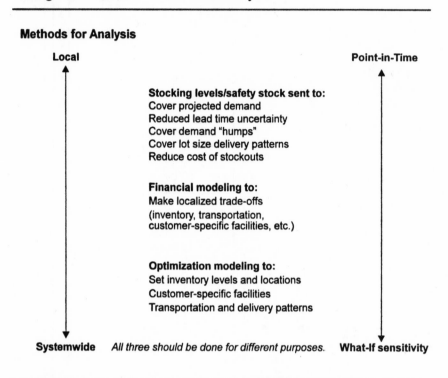

Methods for Analysis

Local   Point-in-Time

Stocking levels/safety stock sent to:
Cover projected demand
Reduced lead time uncertainty
Cover demand "humps"
Cover lot size delivery patterns
Reduce cost of stockouts

Financial modeling to:
Make localized trade-offs
(inventory, transportation,
customer-specific facilities, etc.)

Optimization modeling to:
Set inventory levels and locations
Customer-specific facilities
Transportation and delivery patterns

Systemwide   *All three should be done for different purposes.*   What-If sensitivity

Source: Christopher Gopal and Gerry Cahill. *Logistics in Manufacturing.* Homewood, IL: Richard D. Irwin, Inc., 1992.

levels of customer satisfaction, and the cost of stockouts can be high in terms of lost sales and goodwill. Hence, the key to effective inventory management is the setting of a reasonable balance between carrying costs and service levels. This is a dynamic relationship; as operational cycle times shrink, the inventory required to maintain planned service levels decreases. The ultimate vision, of course, is no lead time and no inventory. Many companies do, however, set inventory policies and fill rates based on the profit impact of service and the probability of the customer buying elsewhere.

Figure 2.10 illustrates some of the guidelines used in setting inventory policies and fill rates by product class and customer segment mix. This

FIGURE 2–10
Guidelines to Setting Inventory Policies and Fill Rates by Product Class—Customer Segment Mix

Customer Seg-	Product Classes	Phase-Out	Mature/Ongoing — Low Margin	Mature/Ongoing — Medium Margin	Mature/Ongoing — High Margin	Ramp-Up/ Introductions
Mass	High competitive	Bleed stock Cover with NPI	Higher inventory Limited expediting	High inventory Limited expediting	High inventory Expedite	Highest inventory High expediting
Account	Low leverage over customer	EOL planning			Low inventory Make to order	Higher inventory Make to order
Account	Contractual	Make to order	Make to order	Make to order		
Account	High leverage over customer	EOL planning Bleed stock	Low-higher inventory Limited expediting back order	Higher inventory Limited expediting back order	Higher inventory Expedite	High inventory High expediting
Mass	Low competitive	Bleed stock		Lower-higher inventory Limited expediting back order	Higher inventory Expedite back order	High inventory Expedite
Account	Captive	EOL planning	Low inventory Limited expediting back order			

Customer Probability of Buying Elsewhere

Profit Impact →

Source: Christopher Gopal and Gerry Cahill. *Logistics in Manufacturing.* Homewood, IL: Richard D. Irwin, Inc., 1992.

implies, of course, that some customers (and channels, where channels, such as distributors, are the customers) are more important than others and that different inventory deployment strategies can exist for products at different points in their life cycles (products being phased out, mature/ongoing products, and ramp-up/new products). It is far too expensive to treat *customer excellence* (and high customer service levels) as a blank check for all classes of customers, channels, and products. If the probability of the customer buying elsewhere (owing to frequent stockouts) is deemed to be high (those segments that are highly competitive or where little leverage over the customer exists), high levels of inventory are often required. As the importance of product availability in the buying decision increases, as in the case of new computer models, this high inventory is often coupled with high levels of expediting to maximize product availability. For low margin, mature products sold to captive or less competitive segments, a cost-effective strategy would include low inventory levels, very limited expediting, and a greater reliance on backorders as a means to fill demand. Figure 2.10 actually represents a continuum on which higher costs are incurred to achieve competitive service levels in highly competitive markets for high margin products, while lower costs are required for those customer segments with little competition for lower margin products.

The other half of the inventory strategy equation is inventory deployment across the logistics network. This typically involves modeling the network, cycle times, and demand patterns for the optimum stocking locations (see Figure 2.11) and explicitly considers the cost of expediting versus the cost of stocking. Lower inventory levels (to a certain extent) can be bought at high expediting costs. One equipment manufacturer reduced its inventory levels for certain products by promising two-day delivery anywhere in the country. It achieved this by using an overnight shipping service and partly offsetting the charges incurred by building some of the shipping costs into the delivered price. The balance was absorbed as a cost of doing business.

These trade-offs make inventory deployment a complex issue. Keys to its effective management are developing a quick response supply chain, excellent supply-demand planning, and ad hoc pipeline inventory management to respond to rapidly changing customer requirements. These require a culture change and a shift in operating values—from *cost-based reaction* to *time- and response-based competition.*

FIGURE 2–11
Inventory Deployment—Modeling the Network

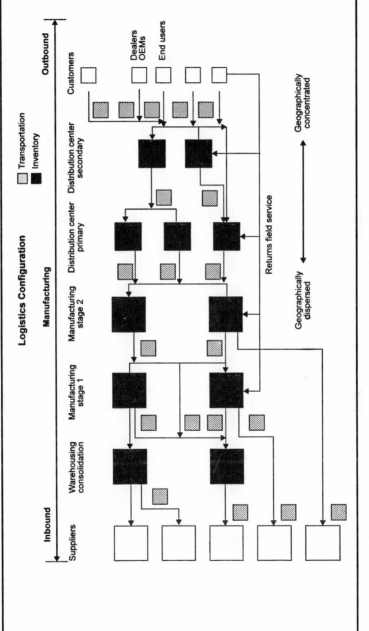

Source: Christopher Gopal and Gerry Cahill. *Logistics in Manufacturing*. Homewood, IL: Richard D. Irwin, Inc., 1992.

Information Technology Strategy

Information technology (IT) is the link that binds the supply chain together, and its use in enabling the logistics and distribution processes can differentiate successful companies from less successful ones. IT must be aligned with corporate strategy and utilized as a key enabler in cross-functional processes to obtain customer delight. Information technology strategy and planning is a major subject in its own right. Chapter 7 in this text discusses the applications and planning issues at a tactical level for integrated distribution.

COMPREHENSIVE IMPLEMENTATION PLANNING

Most well-formulated strategies fail because of poor implementation planning and execution. Implementation planning must encompass change management, information technology migration plans, performance measurement and tracking, schedules, milestones, and responsibilities.

INTEGRATION

This chapter enhances the theme of integration. It illustrates the nature of distribution within its overall context—the supply chain perspective. While subsequent chapters deal with distribution itself, the thread running through this book and the CIRM series involves enterprisewide integration. The logistics strategy encompasses the entire supply chain, of which distribution is a major part. The policies for distribution management are derived from, and driven by, the primary components of logistics strategy. These distribution issues are discussed briefly earlier in this chapter and are summarized in Figure 2.12.

The issues vary in their impact and complexity, depending on the nature of the industry, product, competition, and scope of operations. Nevertheless, they represent the imperatives imposed on integrated distribution by the marketplace and by industry dynamics, and they will be addressed throughout the remainder of this book.

FIGURE 2–12
Distribution Management Issues Driven from Logistics Strategy

These Components of Logistics Strategy

Drives these distribution management issues

Configuration/Network Strategy	Coordination/Organization Strategy	Customer Service Strategy	Integrated Inventory Strategy	Information Technology Strategy
Warehouse management	Role of distribution managers (physical distribution, traffic, warehousing, MIS) in the organization	Manage to service levels	Inventory planning and feedback to supply chain	Selection, acquisition and maintenance
Types of distribution centers	Authority	Evaluate customer base for delivery prioritization	Optimization models for deployment	DRP
Regional, satellite, break-bulk, etc.	Span of control	Field service systems and turnaround	Networkwide deployment to support customer service and marketing strategies	Warehouse management
Their mission and location	Integration of DRP with enterprise materials planning	Customer/market delivery preferences	Stocking locations, levels, mix, etc.	AS/RS
Transportation/traffic management	Planning committee	Lot sizes, frequency, delivery patterns to cost trade-offs		EDI standards
Routing	Ownership of regional forecasts			Transportation/route management
Carrier evaluation and selection				Financial/costing systems
Transportation modes and lanes				Advanced technologies such as expert systems, telecommunications, and microsystems
Outsourcing				
In-house vs. contract carriers				
Company-owned and managed distribution vs. third-party contractors and value-added freight forwarders				
International shipping rules, regulations, tax, and transfer price regulations				

43

LESSONS FOR MANAGERS

The theme of this chapter is the same as the theme of the previous chapter, this book, and the CIRM series—integration within the supply chain and the enterprise. The key lesson is that distribution cannot be operated or managed successfully in isolation. To be effective and competitive, distribution operations must be aligned with supply chain operations and must be consistent with the overall supply chain strategy of the firm. To achieve this alignment, distribution managers must participate in the overall supply chain strategic planning process, including the development of a vision for the supply chain, its mission, goals, and market-based performance measures. Distribution goals and measures that are consistent with the overall direction must, in turn, be developed. Planning for effective distribution operations must include analysis of the cost-service trade-offs to determine the best customer service level and inventory management policies. Every distribution decision involves some cost-service level trade-off.

Distribution managers must be aware of the ramifications of these trade-offs and their impact on overall supply chain strategies and operations. This requires an understanding of the entire spectrum of distribution decisions within the supply chain and the trade-offs inherent in each decision. In turn, this requires data for use in analyzing the trade-offs, expertise in making decisions based on the analysis, and consultation with other functions in the supply chain prior to making the trade-off decisions. These business requirements represent a shift in the role and perspective of the traditional distribution functional manager. They require a distribution manager with an expanded base of knowledge, responsibility, and perspective on the integrated supply chain. While this text provides an integrated distribution perspective, certification in Integrated Resource Management is an excellent way to acquire an expanded perspective on all the major functions in the manufacturing organization.

CHAPTER 3

ORDER MANAGEMENT

Order management is a recently recognized business process in integrated manufacturing and distribution. Its purpose is to plan and monitor all the activities necessary to satisfy customers who place orders for products and services. Many companies have also concluded that order management should extend to the communication and monitoring of all the internal orders that move products through the company's entire supply chain. Such internal orders include:

- Production orders placed on plants.
- Purchase orders placed on suppliers.
- Inventory replenishment orders between the echelons of inventory in the distribution network.

As illustrated in Figure 3.1, order management begins with the receipt of customer orders. The process then sends the orders, along with order management plans (and schedules) for the completion of delivery, to the best supply sources. Order management monitors both delivery performance and customer satisfaction throughout the delivery process, concluding with customer acceptance of the products.

Another feature of the order management process is that for the first time, companies see a way to merge two previously separate sets of activities—customer order management and internal supply order management. In traditional manufacturing and distribution operations, one organization and business process managed orders for customers. Usually called order entry or order fulfillment, the process worked only with customer orders, independent of the other process, which worked with internal supply orders—the replenishment orders between manufacturing locations and downstream distribution locations.

Our view of order management encompasses both customer orders and internal supply orders in the same business process. We illustrate this in Figure 3.1 by showing that all product movement, whether to customers or for internal purposes, comes under order management plans.

The importance of order management is heightened as companies come to recognize that their integrated manufacturing and distribution operations must be driven by three fundamental principles:

• Customer satisfaction is paramount. Order management is the means for focusing the company's total manufacturing and distribution efforts on each customer's requirements.

• The entire supply chain must be customer demand-driven. When customer orders drive all product manufacturing and distribution actions, companies can operate with the lowest inventories at all stages of manufacturing and distribution.

• Well coordinated and timely customer deliveries are a competitive advantage. A company's ability to satisfy customers' delivery requirements is as important a competitive capability as product quality. Customers depend on fewer suppliers for their needs and specify stringent delivery service requirements to meet their own manufacturing and customer service goals.

Adopting these principles calls for profound changes in traditional order management processes. Focusing on customer satisfaction calls for every manufacturing and distribution operation to share ownership of every customer order, rather than limiting customer order visibility to just one place in the supply chain. Becoming customer demand-driven revolutionizes the movement of products through the supply chain, shifting the philosophy of many companies from a push to a pull approach. Customer orders *pull* products through the supply chain. Customer demand pull becomes the driving force for all inventory replenishment and production planning processes. Thus, order management becomes the way to initiate all product flows in the supply chain, using customer demand as the starting point.

The pull philosophy, together with an effective order management process, allows a company to achieve the highest possible return on its investment in its integrated distribution network. Order management, under these circum-

FIGURE 3–1
The Purpose of Order Management

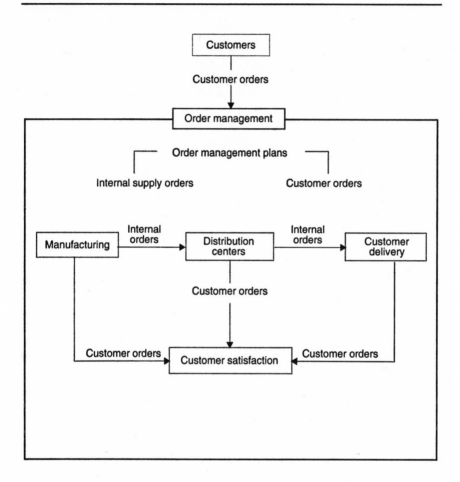

stances, allows companies to match the delivery service levels required by customers with their total supply chain. When this is accomplished, all inventories and production capacities throughout the supply chain can be sized precisely to customer demand. This also places a premium on flexibility in manufacturing operations. When order management connects the entire supply chain to actual customer demand, manufacturers can shift their output among products as demand patterns change and obtain significant competitive advantages in their markets. The advantages arise from being able to offer shorter delivery times, satisfactory service with less inventory, and a lower cost structure for a given manufacturing capacity.

Achieving consistently well-coordinated and timely customer deliveries requires the entire supply chain to have a plan for satisfying every customer order. This *order management plan* provides the company with the means by which to make highly accurate delivery commitments to customers and coordinate the efforts of its entire supply chain to achieve them consistently.

Having an excellent order management process enables the company to achieve important integrated manufacturing and distribution performance objectives, among which are:

- Order to delivery times that meet or exceed customer requirements.

- Order management quality that minimizes missed deliveries and maximizes customer service performance.

- Reduced inventory needs at every stage of the supply chain.

- Increased return on assets, such as plant and distribution center facilities, materials handling equipment, and transportation vehicles, employed in the supply chain.

- Increased capability to build to order in manufacturing locations thereby eliminating significant levels of finished inventory in other parts of the supply chain.

- Reduced total logistics costs across the entire supply chain.

THE ORDER MANAGEMENT PROCESS

Focusing on the role of order management, let us first look at the elements of order management that plan and coordinate customer delivery—*customer order management*. Then we can extend order management's scope to *supply chain order management,* the internal production and inventory replenishment orders that move products through the integrated network to locations other than a customer.

Customer Order Management

Finding effective ways to satisfy many different types of customers, whose product requirements may differ as well, is the key challenge for customer order management. Traditional supply chains, with inflexible manufacturing and distribution components, have had numerous difficulties dealing with today's competitive requirements. It is difficult for them to tailor their products and delivery service to unique customer requirements. They cannot commit to precise delivery times. They cannot coordinate all the components of an order when the order is sourced from several different locations. Equally difficult is sourcing from supply chain locations, such as plants or reserve stocking locations, that are not normally used for customer delivery.

To overcome supply chain inflexibility and other weaknesses, customer order management seeks to pull products from the supply chain according to each customer's unique needs, using all elements of the supply chain simultaneously—sourcing from whatever supply chain location makes sense for the customer in question. To accomplish this we have to expand the traditional definition of *order entry* or *order fulfillment* to the full scope of customer order management.

The difference between order entry and order management is quite large. Traditionally, order entry meant accepting an order and fulfilling it at a single supply source, such as the distribution center assigned to serve a particular customer. In many companies, a single customer order contains order lines that have to go through many different order entry processes to be complete. Order management changes all that. By focusing on the entire customer order and helping to decide which supply sources to involve for each item on the order, order management can plan the coordinated actions of all supply sources to achieve what most customers want—*a simple, consolidated, on-time delivery.*

Further, customer-supply source assignments no longer have to remain fixed. When nominal customer-supply source pairings are planned and used, if the order requires another solution or the nominal supply source is unable to fulfill the order (it has experienced a stock out, for example), order management seeks other supply source options and communicates the customer's needs to them immediately. Order management does not seek approvals for the required actions or go through several layers of distribution outlets in the supply chain. As a result, cycle times and customer delivery times are shorter.

FIGURE 3–2
Steps in Customer Order Management

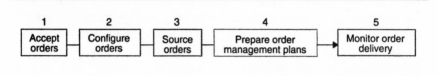

Figure 3.2 illustrates the steps involved in carrying out customer order management, offering some insight into how the job of order management has expanded to meet competitive requirements. Those steps are:

1. *Accept orders*—Order management receives all customer orders from all order streams, including sales representatives, electronic data interchange from customers, telemarketing orders, and any source used by the company, and manages their satisfaction.

2. *Configure orders*—Each customer order consists of a set of products and services necessary to accomplish its delivery. Order management identifies all of these needs even when they are not specifically listed on the order.

3. *Source orders*—Based on the customer's delivery requirements, order management determines the options available to meet them based on the current and expected availability of all the products and services required to complete the delivery.

4. *Prepare order management plans*—Using the source options available and their expected delivery lead times, order management makes a plan for the coordinated customer delivery and communicates that plan to each source selected.

5. *Monitor order delivery*—Order management proactively monitors both the anticipated progress on the customer's order management plan and the actual progress.

The application of each step covers a broad range of integrated distribution capabilities. To understand them let us look at the issues and concerns involved in each step.

FIGURE 3–3
Order Management Accepts All Order Streams

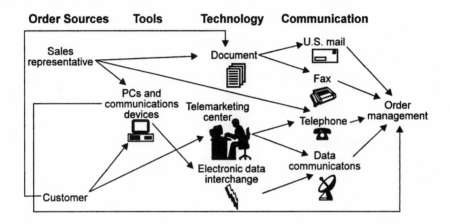

Order Sources   Tools   Technology   Communication

Sales representative

Document

U.S. mail

PCs and communications devices

Fax

Telemarketing center

Telephone

Order management

Electronic data interchange

Data communicatons

Customer

Accept Orders

Today's complex customer environment calls for the company to be able to accept orders from a wide variety of sources using an equally wide range of communications technologies. Companies want to be easy to do business with. Therefore, order management must be able to accept all types of orders regardless of their source or medium of communication. Because customers will choose many ordering methods to reduce their ordering costs, most companies today have concluded that they must be adept at accepting and satisfying orders regardless of how the customer wants to place them. Most companies today are committed to accepting all types of orders from customers. As illustrated in Figure 3.3, companies expect to see:

• Traditional orders prepared by company sales representatives and communicated on paper by mail, fax, or express delivery to a company order management location.

- Orders prepared by sales representatives and transmitted electronically directly to company information systems.

- Orders sent directly from a customer by mail, fax, or express delivery, and orders telephoned in with or without written confirmation.

- Orders sent from a customer by electronic data interchange according to the customer's choice of EDI standard, software and hardware, and communications network

- Orders sent from a customer using information technology provided by the company itself—giving the customer direct access to the company's order management information system, for example.

The order management need is to capture and accept all types of orders with equal ease so they may all be visible at the same time to all elements of the supply chain. It is no longer effective for a company to have many separate order information sources. Companies are consolidating all the order information sources that separately served such distinct parts of the business as product sales, telemarketing sales, catalog sales, after market parts, post-sales supplies, and international sales. Order management will provide just one source for all order information.

Individual company needs may differ depending on the nature of their integrated distribution approach and their customer environment. Companies with multiple distribution centers will no longer want to isolate them so that each center has access to only a subset of all customer orders. Separate systems for different customer or market segments, while helpful in dealing with specialized selling needs, will have to be consolidated at some stage in the order management process. Companies that must coordinate product delivery with installation services (computers, medical equipment, and machine tools, for example) will have to expand their order management scope to capture post-sales and service business.

Configure Orders

In the context of order management, each order consists of the precise set of products and services required to satisfy the customer. Order management must have a complete list to source and plan each product and service element of the order. In many companies, it is not obvious what should be on the list. Delivering or installing products may require parts or supplies that have not previously been written on the order. A good example is the requirement that a service or installation technician be on hand at delivery time. In other instances, what may be written on the order or used in traditional order entry may be only a company's shorthand description of a longer list. For example, the terse order line *gear box* may require installation components that come from a different source—plant, distribution center, or outside vendor. Order management will require that information. Even simple products suffer from this problem. Delivering a case of hospital supplies may require the insertion of special documents in the box or the use of a special label or bar code strip for a particular customer.

A more challenging example arises when the product is made up of several components specially configured or preconfigured for a particular market or stocking location. Order management wants to look deeper into the product configuration just in case the preconfigured item is not available. In some companies the order management process would attempt to acquire the individual components to achieve the desired configuration if that action met the customer's requirements and no preferable solution would do.

As this reveals, order management is highly dependent on the company's overall configuration management philosophy. The need becomes critical when products, such as software and medical devices, are produced in rapidly evolving versions or models. Many companies depend on order management to aid the customer in purchasing either the latest version or one that is compatible with his previous purchases. In these cases, order management must keep close watch on configuration issues and share responsibility for them with engineering or manufacturing organizations.

Source Orders

Order management processes use the company's entire supply chain to identify and choose the most effective sources for satisfying customer orders. Flexibility in satisfying customers is the goal, and there is every reason to consider the entire supply chain's resources when deciding how to satisfy each customer. Under most circumstances the company has determined well in advance those operating policies or rules that tell order management how to satisfy an order. Customers and products are normally assigned to one or more plants or distribution center locations where their orders are filled. Customer service objectives, geographical locations, and the associated costs of transportation, inventory, and facilities usually determine these assignments.

When the entire supply chain is demand-driven, different kinds of rules are used. Rather than relying on sometimes inflexible rules for sourcing orders, the company develops options for each order. For example, some orders may be sourced from a nearby inventory location because their customers require rapid delivery or small quantities. Other orders may bypass a local inventory location and be sourced directly from a plant if their delivery timing allows. If the plant's delivery lead time meets some customers' requirements, then satisfying some orders directly from the plant reduces inventory requirements significantly. Much of the demand uncertainty usually born by inventories near the customer can be reduced or eliminated.

Demand-driven supply chains have allowed some companies, such as personal computer makers, to compete in national markets without any finished inventories at all. It is entirely possible to buy a PC built to your exact specifications, with one- or two-day delivery, through a telephone call to the plant. At the plant, your specifications are transformed immediately into a product configuration that satisfies your needs and can be shipped the same day. Compare the inventories in this supply chain with those needed to support a national network of retail stores offering off-the-shelf PC sales.

In any of these situations, order management defines the potential sources for each item on the order. Progressive order management processes use actual product availability status to determine the options rather than relying on historical expectations. They do this through real-time direct connections to inventory positions throughout the supply chain and similar visibility of production schedules. In seeking potential sources, order management compares customer requirements with the product availability offered by the source and estimates the cost of satisfying the order from each optional source. Costs are important because they affect product and customer profitability. Costs usually include transportation costs, consolidation costs, and costs incurred to fill an order from each optional source.

Prepare Order Management Plans

With a single supply source or when supply sources are few, sourcing the order is tantamount to initiating its shipment. Such is the case with highly centralized integrated distribution operations such as those used by catalog sellers and makers of machine tools, automobiles, and home appliances.

Manufacturers of consumer products, such as groceries, consumer electronics, and health and beauty aids, also use integrated distribution networks that, by design, offer few options. Their sales channels are so vast that they must maintain extensive distribution networks to achieve rapid inventory turnover. They have little need for comparing options, but their order management processes still reflect the flexibility in sourcing that their integrated supply chains make available. Then they can deal with exceptions, such as unexpected stockouts or unforeseen breakdowns in equipment, that arise from time to time.

In other companies, especially those whose products are complex (computers, machine tools, and medical imaging equipment, for example) an order management plan serves to coordinate all the elements of customer delivery. The plan, much like a project management plan, includes the complete schedule of product shipments from their respective sources and all the services required to complete the delivery. As shown in Figure 3.4, those services include any needed shipments, consolidations, pre-delivery services, and delivery and installation at the customer's desired location. In some situations, the order management plan also includes customer training, post-sales support services (such as maintenance service), or continuing supplies or parts shipment

One of the advantages of an effective order management process is that plans are based on the actual availability of supply, rather than estimates or promises. Order management seeks to tap directly into the inventories or production capacities of the supply sources, obtaining certain commitments of supply. This means that highly accurate delivery times can be offered to customers with confidence. It also means that the time to communicate order requirements throughout the supply chain is fast, sometimes instantaneous. As a result, total lead time for customer order delivery can be short, a competitive advantage in many markets.

Making an order management plan also involves communicating the plan to the supply sources that will satisfy the components of the plan. This involves communicating part of the customer's order to each place in the supply chain responsible for shipping a product or providing a service such as transportation or installation. Communication is usually accomplished via data communications networks that provide almost instant and simultaneous communication to all supply sources. This simultaneous communication means that a process that previously might have required a number of sequential steps over many days can now occur in a matter of seconds.

FIGURE 3–4
An Order Management Plan

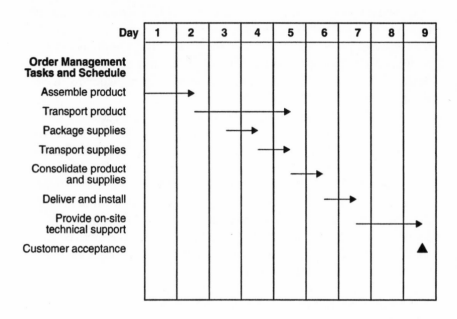

Day	1	2	3	4	5	6	7	8	9

Order Management Tasks and Schedule

Assemble product
Transport product
Package supplies
Transport supplies
Consolidate product and supplies
Deliver and install
Provide on-site technical support
Customer acceptance

Under these circumstances, many supply sources no longer have to wait for the completion of other tasks before they can begin their work. For example, in transportation scheduling, a truck manifest can be planned well before the shipment is ready, because both the transportation planners and the product suppliers are working with the same order management plan and can see precisely what the other is planning and whether a delay or change has occurred in the upstream or downstream activities surrounding them.

Another striking advantage of order management planning and communication is that order management plans can be capable of reaching deeply into supply sources' management systems to reduce communication time and eliminate many traditional steps found at the interfaces between supply sources. Companies are designing order management processes with some of the following features in mind:

- Order management plans can initiate production by placing an order directly on the manufacturing production schedule.

- Where products are in warehouses, order management can communicate an order directly to the picking operation, bypassing traditional order entry processes which held up orders for hours or days while picking was planned and scheduled.

- In high velocity inventory situations, order management can place an order on product yet to arrive at the receiving dock and have the product routed directly to shipping, bypassing the stocking and picking of that product.

- For service operations, order management can directly access the daily and hourly schedules of service technicians to reserve a time slot.

- Order management can select a truck route and place the order on the truck's manifest at the same time the order is sent to the warehouse.

The order management plan, besides being the principal way to commit supply sources to the common goal of satisfying customer orders, is the principal management tool for monitoring performance.

Monitor Order Delivery

A key feature of order management is the ability to monitor the order management plan among all its participants and anticipate problems, conflicts, and other circumstances that could put on-time delivery in jeopardy. Using the order management plan, companies proactively obtain input from every involved supply source regarding the status of its contribution to satisfying the customer's requirements. Actual actions taken by supply sources can be compared with planned actions.

When supply sources run into problems, the impact of the problems can be assessed and new actions planned. Depending on the options available to the supply source, the actions of the other participants may be adjusted with a new order management plan. This provides the customer with an update on delivery according to the new plan.

Order management enables the company to monitor all the product movement in the supply chain. This offers supply sources more flexibility in satisfying orders than when they were isolated from all the other orders in the supply chain. Unexpected problems at one supply source can be solved by assessing the opportunities and the costs of using alternate supply sources.

Supply Chain Order Management

Supply chain order management is the equivalent of customer order management for moving products through the supply chain. Figure 3.5 portrays the kinds of orders that normally move through the supply chain. Here the supply sources are upstream components of the supply chain, such as manufacturing and national distribution centers. Their customers are such downstream components of the supply chain as regional distribution centers and local customer support inventories. The orders that move products among these supply chain components are sometimes called *internal supply chain orders* or just *internal orders*.

Supply chain order management is carried out using exactly the same steps as customer order management:

1. Accept orders.
2. Configure orders.
3. Source orders.
4. Prepare order management plans.
5. Monitor order delivery.

Rather than basing delivery requirements on the requirements of individual customer orders, however, supply chain order management depends on a wealth of logistics and inventory management rules to govern the timing, quantity, and other specifications of internal orders. Supply chain order management works in the company's total logistics management environment to execute the steps that move all products through the entire supply chain.

Figure 3.6 illustrates the process of supply chain order management with pull replenishment policies. Supply chain order management continuously monitors the inventory levels at each location. As customer orders are satisfied, supply chain order management checks to see if those orders necessitate pulling more inventory from upstream supply sources. If needed, supply chain order management initiates the movement by creating the internal

FIGURE 3–5
Supply Chain Order Management

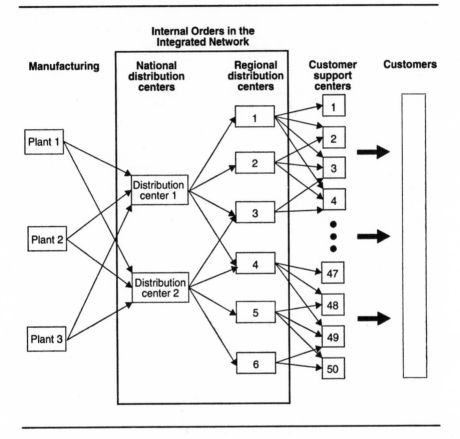

order for the move. This in turn may initiate pulling product from a further upstream supply source such as a manufacturing plant or a vendor.

All the specifications of these supply chain orders can be developed by supply chain management using the company's inventory replenishment policies and its production scheduling policies. Inventory or production scheduling policies determine quantities and supply sources for all orders moving in the supply chain. This means that order management can keep track of every supply chain order and use the information to plan all customer order deliveries.

FIGURE 3–6
Supply Order Management with Pull Replenishment Rules

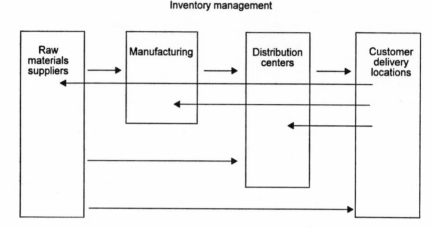

Inventory management

Transportation management

◄───── Supply chain internal orders with pull replenishment
───► Supply chain deliveries

Other policies, such as transportation schedules, determine internal order delivery timing. Production schedules provide access to manufacturing capacity when the internal order is for products sourced at a plant. Purchasing agreements do the same when the supply source is an outside supplier or vendor.

LESSONS FOR MANAGERS

The order management process has profound implications for the way companies work. Applying the process motivates companies to answer some very tough questions:

• Who is in charge of the order management process?

- Which parts of the company are accountable for order management performance?

- How can traditional conflicts between manufacturing, marketing, and distribution be resolved to make the order management process work smoothly?

- How can customer satisfaction goals be transformed into sound performance measures that apply effectively to manufacturing and distribution simultaneously?

- How do you bring new products or new customers into the existing order management process without a loss of performance?

The way to answer these questions is to take a process-oriented view of business performance. First, every organization in the supply chain must buy into the order management process. Manufacturing must determine what it means to be customer demand-driven. Marketing must determine what customer satisfaction means and what quantitative performance levels will achieve it. Distribution must design and operate a network of locations that offer the flexibility to satisfy customers from any or all locations if necessary.

Second, manufacturing, marketing, and distribution must share the same goals—customer satisfaction and order management process performance goals. They ought to agree that well-coordinated and on-time customer deliveries are everyone's responsibility, because achieving this is a shared critical success factor for every organization in the company. Performance evaluation and compensation policies should be aligned with these shared goals.

Third, an enormous amount of knowledge must be shared across all the organizations involved with order management. Customer service workers must understand production processes. Manufacturing workers must understand customers. Distribution workers must understand production processes, inventory policies, and customer requirements.

Fourth, and probably most critical to sustained order management success, all resources (capital, budgetary, and human) should be allocated in a single process across the entire supply chain. Resource allocation, whether for projects, new equipment, or staffing, should be justified on the basis of optimizing customer satisfaction. Otherwise some of the most important investments—those that remove the traditional boundaries between supply chain organizations—never get the attention they deserve.

CHAPTER 4

THE INTEGRATED MANUFACTURING AND DISTRIBUTION NETWORK

This chapter covers the company's integrated manufacturing and distribution network, which is illustrated in Figure 4.1. This network is made up of the total set of manufacturing, distribution, and customer delivery locations and facilities through which the company moves products to satisfy customers. Our focus is on the mission of the network, its design, and its operation. These three characteristics of the network will explain its competitive role in the company and the contribution it makes toward achieving company-wide goals for customer satisfaction.

Integrated manufacturing and distribution networks are designed and constructed to integrate and serve three fundamental processes in a company: manufacturing, distribution, and customer delivery. From the customer's point of view, these are the processes that add value and make for customer satisfaction. The way in which a company designs and uses its network to achieve customer satisfaction depends on which of the three processes the company decides to pursue and operate. The choices represent the places or activities in the supply chain where the company believes it can add value profitably. Figure 4.1 also illustrates the value added at each location in the integrated manufacturing and distribution network.

Usually a company's decisions regarding where in the network it can add value profitably are based on the following:

- *Business environment and strategy*—The products the company chooses to sell, the competitors it has in the marketplace, and the

FIGURE 4–1
The Integrated Manufacturing and Distribution Network

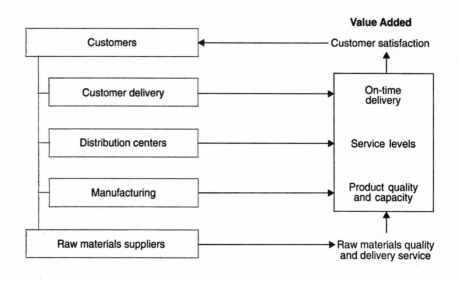

competitive strategies it follows to market and sell products to the customers it believes want to buy them.

- *Financial resources*—The cash, debt, and equity available to the company to invest in network assets (facilities and equipment), the working capital available to invest in inventories, and the operating budget available to operate the network.

- *Management strengths*—The knowledge and skills the company has which help determine which segments of its products' marketing channels the company will participate in. Is the company a manufacturer alone or a manufacturer and distributor? Will the company serve the product's end user or sell the product to others who have decided to fulfill that role in the marketing channel?

Most companies see the above three factors as essential in defining a *strategic business unit* or SBU. An SBU is a complete business whose profit and return on investment can be measured. An SBU is a business unit that has well-defined competition among the same group of customers for the same types of products and a unit whose financial decisions are made independently of other corporate activities or strategic business units. Most large corporations consist of a number SBUs. For example, General Electric Corporation is made up of more than 100 SBUs. Each SBU has different products and customers, and each has its own competitors.

For our purposes in this chapter, we will look at the integrated manufacturing and distribution network needs of a single SBU. Our SBU could be one of many that share a single corporation-wide network. We will not go into the special issues and concerns that exist when a single shared network must accommodate the needs of many SBUs.

In considering the mission, design, and operation of an integrated manufacturing and distribution network, three fundamental principles should guide managers' decisions concerning the network:

1. *Satisfy customers*—The network exists, first and foremost, to satisfy customer requirements for timely product delivery. Each manufacturing, distribution, and customer delivery facility is part of one continuous supply chain whose singular objective is customer satisfaction.

2. *Achieve acceptable return on investment*—The assets (network facilities and equipment) and inventory required to satisfy customers depend almost exclusively on the design of the network—the number and location of network facilities. Network design must optimize customer satisfaction with the lowest possible investment in inventory and facilities.

3. *Integrate the network*—Each facility and location in the network must add value to the product, value in the eyes of the customer. Figure 4.1 shows the basic value-added steps in the network from the customer's point of view. The network must be operated as one single value-adding supply chain, rather than a sequence of separate operations, their own independent objectives and performance measures. Rather than interface the elements of the network, managers want to integrate them and resolve all the potential conflicts that could arise among the network elements.

COMPONENTS OF THE NETWORK

To describe the mission, design, and operation of the network, we must understand that the network consists of more than just plants and warehouses. It includes the company's choices for:

- *The types, numbers, and locations of facilities*—The value-adding facilities that provide manufacturing, distribution, and customer delivery services in the network.
- *The product flow processes*—The processes used to manage the flow of product between all facilities in the network and the performance measures used to evaluate customer satisfaction.
- *The return on investment objectives*—The company's objectives for investing in network assets, including inventories.

Network facility types are described below. We will discuss product flow processes in Chapter 5. Return on investment objectives are covered in the network design section of this chapter.

Network Facilities

Three types of facilities are found in an integrated manufacturing and distribution network:

- *Manufacturing*—Facilities where value is added through the conversion of raw materials and labor into products whose value, quality, and cost are desired by customers.
- *Distribution*—Facilities where value is added by keeping products or consolidating different products at a location that is close enough to customers in distance or time to offer delivery service levels that satisfy customers' requirements; or facilities whose locations, relative to manufacturing and customer delivery processes, offer value by enabling lower transportation costs.
- *Customer delivery*—Facilities which add value by carrying out the order management process (described in Chapter 3) to assure that customer order deliveries, made up of both products and services, can be carried out to satisfy customers.

FIGURE 4-2
Network Facilities Integration for Customer Satisfaction

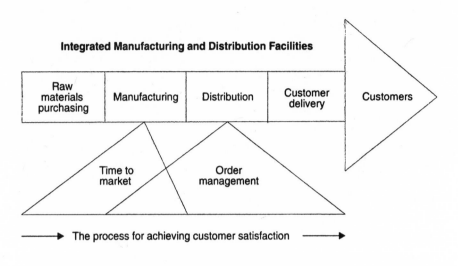

Integrated Manufacturing and Distribution Facilities

| Raw materials purchasing | Manufacturing | Distribution | Customer delivery | Customers |

Time to market

Order management

The process for achieving customer satisfaction

Figure 4.2 illustrates how these three types of facilities are integrated to achieve customer satisfaction. Two business processes serve to integrate the network—*time to market* and *order management*. Order management was covered earlier in Chapter 3. That process serves to connect the entire network to customers by planning all the steps required to satisfy an order. Time to market, as used in this context, is the business process that allows the company to manufacturer quality products within a time frame that satisfies customers with a minimum of resources such as inventory, labor, and plant capacity.

In many companies, each type of facility is in a different geographical location. In many others, however, two or more of these facility types are co-located. For example, the manufacturing and distribution facilities may share the same building or campus. Manufacturing and customer delivery facilities may be in the same building when distribution processes are not performed by the company in its business environment.

Manufacturing Facilities

Manufacturing facilities add value by converting raw materials into quality products that customers want to buy. In the integrated manufacturing and distribution network, manufacturing facilities have the broader responsibility of making those quality products at just the right time. If they produce them too early or in quantities that exceed customer demand, undesired inventories accumulate adding to investment requirements for working capital and increasing the risk that customer demand will not materialize. If manufacturing produces products too late, the company will not be able to deliver customer orders in the required time. Market share could be lost.

These requirements for timely production have become the most important goals for most manufacturing facilities. To achieve them, manufacturers are turning to a wealth of productive concepts that offer competitive advantages in time to market and, when executed well, other advantages such as cost reduction and flexibility. Some of these concepts are:

- *Just-in-time operations*—Having raw materials delivered directly to their point of use in the plant on the same day they are needed so that they are available just in time for required production operations; and performing those production operations only when customer orders dictate, in response to a customer demand-driven supply chain.

- *Build-to-order*—Postponing the assembly or final configuration of products until customer orders require such operations, thereby reducing the need for finished inventories of many different products or configurations.

- *Focused factories*—Designing and building factories focused on the production of a single product or a small group of closely related products rather than multiproduct factories where the complexity of the product mix makes it difficult to segregate products and apply JIT or build-to-order processes.

- *Pull production modes*—Using production schedules that are based entirely on customer driven demand, abandoning standard lot sizes that represent historical demand averages and assume that inventories are acceptable in the supply chain.

- *Electronic data interchange*—Receiving and transmitting orders, order status, shipment advice, and all other business transactions by computer-to-computer communications, speeding up the process and eliminating redundant data entry and paperwork.

Distribution Facilities

Distribution facilities add value by making products available to customers at locations or in quantities that offer levels of service—product availability—which meet customer requirements. They also add value by offering space and services that help reduce transportation expenses, usually through the ability to transport full truckload quantities for much of the supply chain distance between manufacturing and customer delivery locations. Distribution facilities sometimes offer services such as product packaging, labeling, and final assembly that add value when such processes can be postponed until the product has left the manufacturing facility.

In the integrated manufacturing and distribution network, distribution facilities serve as temporary locations for products that are on their way from manufacturing to customers. They help to manage the total flow of product through the supply chain. This is quite different from the traditional role of distribution locations. Companies previously looked upon distribution facilities as places from which to manage inventory rather than the flow of product. Today, the requirement is to move the product toward the customer in one continuous flow, eliminating all disruptions.

To achieve this objective, distribution facilities are designed and operated using many of the following practices:

- *Stockless distribution*—The distribution facility serves as a way station in the customer delivery process. Product arrives in one form (in consolidated shipments for many customers, for example), and the distribution facility adds value by changing that form (to individual customer orders, for example) and converting the flow of product so it can keep moving in the supply chain. Inventories are not kept at the distribution facility.
- *Final assembly points*—Distribution facilities receive the unfinished product and complete the assembly process only for specific

customer orders, thereby postponing adding value until exact customer requirements are known.

- *Cross docking*—Customer orders arrive ready to be delivered. The distribution facility serves as the point of transfer from one type of transportation (long-haul full truckload, for example) to another (local delivery or route trucks, for example).

- *Customer logistics centers*—Distribution facilities take over the complete logistics function for their customers, making local deliveries, repackaging, labeling, and holding all stocks not yet wanted at their customers' locations. The facility takes customer orders and maintains all information about usage and future needs.

- *Automated storage and retrieval*—Using engineered systems, which move unattended through the warehouse to put-away and pick product, distribution facilities are speeding up customer order filling.

- *Warehouse management systems*—Working with information transmitted by radio, picking and put away instructions are automatically displayed on warehouse workers' forklift trucks telling them where to go and what to do for all product movements. Bar code scanners automatically route products via conveyor belts, taking them from one location to another without human intervention, sometimes consolidating different products for a customer or for a delivery vehicle.

- *Electronic data interchange*—All information needed for distribution facility operations is sent from one computer to another, eliminating duplicate data entry and speeding up the process. Customers send their orders, manufacturing receives orders from the distribution facility, and replenishment orders are automatically placed within the supply chain.

Customer Delivery Facilities

Customer delivery facilities are a new concept in integrated manufacturing and distribution networks. They consist of the facilities, people, and vehicles that perform the final delivery of products to customers. The most illustrative examples lie in such products as snack foods, health and beauty aids, mass merchandise products, office equipment, and computers. These products share the common customer requirement that the delivery process cover much more than simply leaving the product on the customer's receiving dock. They include a substantial amount of value-added service that benefits both the seller and the customer.

Store-door deliveries in the grocery industry exhibit a full range of value-added services for the customer and the seller. Consider the driver of a route delivery truck. His truck, the product on the truck, and the order management process he carries out at each customer location are, together, a well-defined customer delivery facility. They just happen to move around together.

Once at his customer's location, the grocery or convenience store, the driver inspects his display area and immediately enters restocking quantities on his hand-held computing device to bring the shelf stock up to desired and attractive levels. His computer contains all the software needed to determine his customer's order quantities, prices, discounts, and other allowances. After restocking the shelves, he can transmit, directly from his truck, sales data for each customer. That information is used to restock his delivery truck when it returns to his base and to make sales reports available immediately to the company.

The installation of office equipment, such as copiers and computers, uses a different type of customer delivery facility. This customer delivery facility is assembled at the customer's location. It brings with it all the people, equipment, training, and services needed to satisfy the customer's order. Different customer orders require different delivery facilities. The order sets the requirements for the customer delivery facility—its location and equipment, parts, supplies, and personnel needs.

As companies realize that their integrated manufacturing and distribution networks must extend into their customers' businesses, they are employing processes like the two outlined above. These processes, now employed as natural parts of the network, provide the following benefits:

- A detailed understanding of each customer's requirements and the ability to meet them without undue cost or time requirements.
- A way to customize distribution and delivery for important customers without giving up any of the economies of scale, such as regional warehouses and distant manufacturing facilities, that other facilities in the network offer.
- Competitive advantages through excellent customer service, adding value to achieve sustained customer loyalty.

• The flexibility to implement changes in customer delivery requirements at any point in the delivery process.

THE NETWORK'S MISSION AND OPERATION

A company's collection of manufacturing, distribution, and customer delivery facilities makes up a rather diverse set of activities and business processes. What is it that ties them together? What allows the company to coordinate the operations that take place within and among these locations? The answers to these fundamental management questions lie in understanding the mission of the integrated manufacturing and distribution network. Looking at the network's mission gives us an opportunity to view all the facilities and locations as one single business process. We can focus on its contribution to the competitive strength of the company.

Many companies state the mission of the network in one sentence:

Achieve customer satisfaction at the lowest possible operating cost and capital investment.

If we were to take apart this sentence and evaluate the assumptions behind it, we might first concentrate on the key words or phrases—achieve, customer satisfaction, and lowest possible cost. The first key word, *achieve*, is an objective-oriented word. It refers to business objectives. *Customer satisfaction* is something that can be measured. We measure how well we achieve our objective by observing customer satisfaction. *Lowest possible cost* is a strategy-oriented phrase. It tells how we plan to achieve our objective.

Notice that this mission statement focuses the network's goals on a single performance measure, customer satisfaction, that can be shared by all activities in the network. The network's mission could also be the sum of individual manufacturing performance and distribution performance goals. The single customer satisfaction goal helps consolidate all of the individual goals traditionally used to drive the performance of the individual components of the network. The network's goals are the same as the company's goals. With a customer-driven mission, each manufacturing, distribution, and customer delivery location must examine how its operations and performance affect the single goal of customer satisfaction. In this way all the individual goals of manufacturing facilities and distribution facilities become linked.

With customer satisfaction as the network's goal, it becomes increasingly important to understand how network operations and performance influence customer satisfaction. Inherent in that understanding is how each manufacturing, distribution, and customer delivery facility contributes to achieving customer satisfaction. So understanding the network's mission means understanding the following characteristics of the network:

- What constitutes customer satisfaction?
- How does the integrated manufacturing and distribution network help achieve customer satisfaction?
- How does each manufacturing, distribution, and customer delivery facility contribute to customer satisfaction?
- What are the operating and capital costs of the network?

Customer Satisfaction

Customer satisfaction is the most basic, and the most powerful, performance measure any company can use. Customers are satisfied when all their expectations for a product and the services that accompany the product are met all the time. Satisfying customers is the total goal of the company. Different parts of the company and different business processes all have contributions to make to achieving customer satisfaction. Generally, the roles and responsibilities of different company organizations or processes are:

- *Marketing*—Identify customers and their needs, design products that meet those needs, encourage demand through product differentiation, and determine profitable ways to reach desired market segments with sales efforts and product delivery processes.
- *Product development*—Create products in which customers see value that matches or exceeds the total cost of the product to the customer.
- *Supplier management*—Develop relationships and performance measurements that give the company access to the quality raw materials and services needed to produce its products.
- *Production operations*—Produce products with consistent quality to meet customer requirements—products whose costs yield adequate

profit to satisfy company cash flow and return on investment objectives.

• *Order management*—Plan and monitor all activities needed to satisfy customer orders with on-time and complete delivery.

• *Integrated network operations*—Move products through manufacturing, distribution, and customer delivery facilities to satisfy customer demand in the shortest possible time and at the lowest possible cost.

Customers are satisfied only when all their requirements are met. It is an all or nothing proposition. Product quality requirements must be accompanied by quality delivery services. The integrated manufacturing and distribution network provides nearly all the services that usually accompany the product. A few services are found in other business processes such as post-sales product maintenance, billing, credit, and parts sales. What the customer sees most frequently are network services that bring the product to the customer.

As managers become oriented to customer satisfaction as a pervasive performance measure, they sometimes realize that customer satisfaction may not be enough to allow them to achieve their business goals. If all competitors in a market segment provide equal customer satisfaction, one or more of them should see an opportunity to gain a competitive advantage by offering something more that customers value. The strategy could be *innovation*—changing the cost-value relationship customers see in the product or the services that accompany the product. Another strategy could be offering products and services that influence customers to raise their expectations for all competitors. Either way, companies can gain a sustained competitive advantage when they continuously refine the meaning of customer satisfaction. Successful competitors know that it is not enough simply to be familiar with their customers' expectations today. They must lead their customers to greater expectations only they are prepared to satisfy.

The Network's Contribution to Customer Satisfaction

Focusing on the contribution of the integrated network, the elements of customer satisfaction that the network provides include:

• A complete integration of all the value-added processes in manufacturing and distribution that bring a product to the customer.

- Accurate and consistent predictions of delivery times for all customer orders.

- Accurate and complete orders for exactly what the customer wants, when she wants it, and where she wants it.

- Short delivery lead times, usually measured in hours or days rather than weeks and months.

- Complete and timely information about the status of a customer's order.

- Flexibility to respond to changing or special customer requirements.

To further distinguish the network's contribution to customer satisfaction from the contributions of other business processes, such as order management, marketing, and product development, we need to understand the network's role in three important competitive requirements of the business:

- The cycle time to satisfy customer needs for products.

- The performance levels customers require from the network.

- The total network costs to satisfy customer needs.

Customer needs are specific order contents together with their delivery timing and order quality. Order quality, as we saw in Chapter 3, means order-to-delivery cycle times that meet customer requirements. Customers require network performance that shows consistency in meeting delivery requirements. Total network costs are the costs incurred in the manufacturing, distribution, and customer delivery facilities used by the company.

Network Cycle Time

Let's look first at the cycle time to satisfy customer needs. We are concerned about the time it takes products to move through the entire manufacturing and distribution network to satisfy customer needs. Typically, companies measure this as the total elapsed time from a change in product demand volume or rate until the entire network is ready to satisfy the demand. This cycle time, as illustrated in Figure 4.3, consists of three components:

- Production process time.

- Supply process time.

- Order management process time.

FIGURE 4–3
Time to Satisfy Customer Needs in the Integrated Network

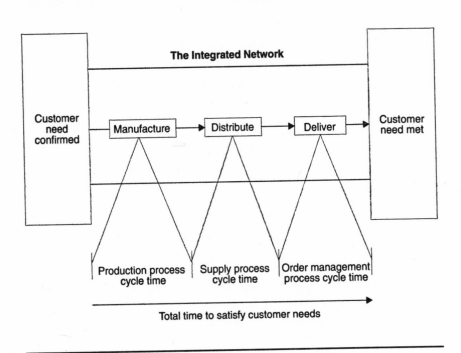

When the product is manufactured to order, the total cycle time is just the production process cycle time plus the order management process cycle time. Where the company uses a network of distribution facilities, we must add the supply process cycle time to obtain the total cycle time to satisfy customer needs. For our discussion, we have omitted another element of time, raw materials acquisition supply time. However, many companies have already implemented ways to eliminate, or at least minimize, raw materials acquisition supply time. They have adopted just-in-time delivery policies or they have made agreements with their vendors to remove all the uncertainty of supply from their processes.

Cycle time to satisfy customer needs is a competitive issue that differentiates one company from another. Customers require the shortest possible cycle times, because shorter cycle times afford them more flexibility in their operations, lower investments of working capital in inventories, and lower operating costs. The integrated network and how it is operated account for nearly all the cycle time customers see. Breaking the total cycle time down among the three processes shown in Figure 4.3, we have:

- *Production process cycle time*—The production process cycle time is the result of the decisions made regarding manufacture of the product. Cycle times are longer when large batches or lots are used. They get much shorter as lot sizes get smaller. They are also influenced by the steps in the production process. Cycle times are longer when the production process begins with raw materials conversion or parts assembly. They are shorter when the production process begins with higher level assemblies or near-ready to sell products that require only a few steps to make them complete and ready to sell.

- *Supply process cycle time*—The supply process cycle time is the result of the number of distribution locations in the network and the transit time between them and the manufacturing locations in the network. Supply cycle time is also a result of the time it takes to move product through an individual distribution facility. That depends on distribution center management decisions which affect how products are received, stored, and selected for shipping in the distribution facility.

- *Order management process cycle time*—Order management cycle time, covered in Chapter 3, consists of the time required to satisfy customer orders from the moment the order is accepted until it is delivered.

The role of the integrated network is to link the manufacturing, distribution, and customer delivery facilities and their internal processes. In Chapter 3, we saw how order management provides the linkage between customer orders and the entire integrated network. Within the network, linkage is based on the same premises—drive product flow with *customer demand*, and use the *pull* philosophy to manage the flow of products within the network.

Figure 4.4 illustrates the opportunity for cycle time reduction when these premises are applied. When the network flow is controlled without

FIGURE 4–4
Linkage in the Network Reduces Cycle Time

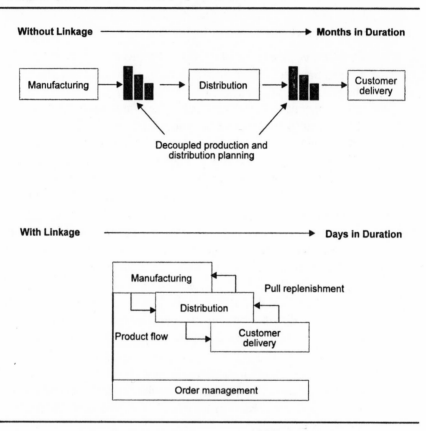

linkage, as in the upper half of Figure 4.4, it can take months for product to move through the entire network. With linkage provided by the pull philosophy and order management processes, cycle times can be reduced to a matter of days.

Network Performance Levels

A second area of contribution to customer satisfaction made by the integrated manufacturing and distribution network is through the network's

FIGURE 4–5
Network Customer Service Level Measures

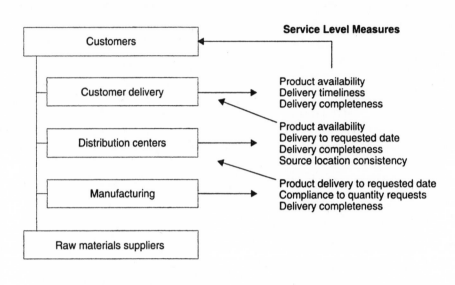

performance in providing what the customer wants, when he wants it, and where he wants it. This performance usually is measured by observing the *customer service level*. Customer service level performance measures differ for each type of facility in the network. For example, Figure 4.5 indicates several types of service level metrics that can be used across the integrated manufacturing and distribution network.

In any facility or location, the most important service level measures are customer delivery service level measures. These should be very similar to customers' requirements for product availability, delivery timeliness, and order completion. Measuring the network's performance in the same terms that customers' requirements are given is the most effective way to measure network performance.

A more extensive description of network performance measurement is provided in Chapter 6.

Network Cost Factors

A third area of contribution to customer satisfaction is the network's ability to achieve customer satisfaction at the lowest possible operating cost and capital investment. When we look at the network as a completely integrated set of facilities and operations put in place to achieve customer satisfaction, we get the chance to add up all the costs and investments required to achieve that satisfaction. We can also see how the network influences the company's overall return on investment in the network.

We will put network costs and investments in context with company costs and capital requirements and then have a closer look at the role of the network in managing company investments by making the right trade-offs to achieve customer satisfaction at the lowest possible operating cost and capital investment.

Every company looks to its integrated manufacturing and distribution network to achieve three results:

- Customer satisfaction.
- Profits.
- Return on investment.

Figure 4.6 illustrates how the network takes responsibility for achieving these results. From the company's point of view, it has three key responsibilities to its owners or shareholders: create customer demand, plan and control operations, and acquire capital. The network has three corresponding responsibilities then: deliver products, operate at the lowest possible cost, and invest in network facilities.

Putting these together we can see how the company's desired results are achieved:

Create Customer Demand + Deliver Products = **Customer Satisfaction**
Customer satisfaction yields a continuing flow
of sales and sales revenue.

Plan and Control Operations + Operate Network at Lowest Cost = **Profits**
Profits yield cash flow and access to capital from debt and
equity sources.

Acquire Capital + Invest in Network Facilities = **Return on Investment**
Return on investment yields a competitive advantage.

FIGURE 4–6
Company Expectations for Network Costs and Investments

Thus, the integrated network is directly involved in providing a competitive advantage for the company. It is equally important in sustaining the revenues and profits that allow the company to finance its growth and increase its net worth.

The components of network operating costs and investment needs are complex and involve numerous trade-offs to achieve customer satisfaction at the lowest possible cost and investment. The components can be classified as variable and fixed costs over a planning horizon and investments in fixed assets and working capital. Figure 4.7 illustrates the typical network costs and investments most companies incur in the operation of their integrated manufacturing and distribution networks. Some components, depending on the form of financing (lease versus purchase, for example) may be either operating costs or investments.

No matter how these costs and investment components are accounted for, the network costs and investments represent management decisions made about three fundamental *costs of customer satisfaction:*

- The cost of manufacturing.
- The cost of transportation.
- The cost of capital for facilities and inventory.

FIGURE 4–7
Network Operating Costs and Investments

Operating Costs		Investments*
Variable Costs	*Fixed Costs*	*Short and Long Term*
Order management	Office space	Manufacturing facilities
Customer delivery	Warehouse space	Distribution facilities
Distribution center operations	Information technology equipment	Customer delivery facilities
Product transportation	Vehicles	Vehicles
Telecommunications		Telecommunications equipment
Interest on working capital for inventory and facilities		Information technology equipment
Consumable supplies		
Personnel		

*Depending on financing options, some costs may be either operating costs or investments.

Every integrated network represents a calculated trade-off among these cost factors to achieve a desired level of customer satisfaction. Just such a trade-off is illustrated in Figure 4.8. Here we see a comparison of manufacturing, transportation, facility, and inventory costs for two different networks. Both networks achieve the same level of customer satisfaction.

Both options serve a national market. Option 1 uses one manufacturing facility, which doubles as a distribution center for the Northeast, for the entire market. Other distribution centers are located in Atlanta and Los Angeles to serve regional markets nearby. Option 2 is different. It has two manufacturing facilities, one in New Jersey and the other in Los Angeles. Both serve as distribution centers. A third distribution center is located in Atlanta. In this simple example, the cost comparison is shown in the bar chart at the right in Figure 4.8.

To achieve the same level of customer satisfaction, Option 1 has a potential manufacturing cost advantage over Option 2, because its manufacturing is consolidated in one location. But that potential advantage is

FIGURE 4-8
Network Cost and Investment Trade-offs

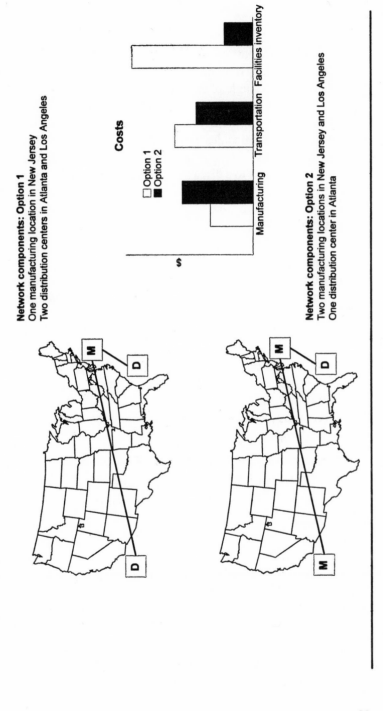

Network components: Option 1
One manufacturing location in New Jersey
Two distribution centers in Atlanta and Los Angeles

Costs

□ Option 1
■ Option 2

Manufacturing   Transportation   Facilities   inventory

$

Network components: Option 2
Two manufacturing locations in New Jersey and Los Angeles
One distribution center in Atlanta

overshadowed by the higher transportation and inventory costs needed to service three distribution centers from a single manufacturing location. Additional inventory is required in Option 1 to provide for the longer transit times between the single plant and the distribution centers. Option 2 yields a lower total cost because transportation and inventory costs are lower for the two plants serving widely separated markets in the East and the West.

While most companies explore options that are much more complex than the ones shown in the example in Figure 4.8, the trade-offs are quite similar. This leads us to a discussion of network design in the section below.

NETWORK DESIGN

Few companies design their integrated manufacturing and distribution networks from scratch. A company must continue to operate while its business environment and strategies evolve over time. The evolution of the business environment involves constant changes in competitive structure and sometimes discontinuous changes in what constitutes customer satisfaction.

Our focus for describing network design issues will be the process of *transition*. However, the same concepts may be applied to the design of a totally new network for a new company or a new strategic business unit in an existing company.

The transition we emphasize consists of the following cycle of management processes, as illustrated in Figure 4.9:

- Understanding and monitoring the evolving business environment.
- Determining the optimal network to achieve customer satisfaction at the lowest possible cost and investment.
- Determining the gap between the current network and the optimal one.
- Deciding if the gap is large enough to warrant change and if the cost of that change is currently affordable.
- If the change is affordable, developing a transition plan to make it.
- Executing the transition plan and monitoring results against the evolving business environment.

The *network transition cycle* brings together the evolving business environment, the company's strategies for products, markets, and invest-

FIGURE 4–9
The Network Transition Cycle

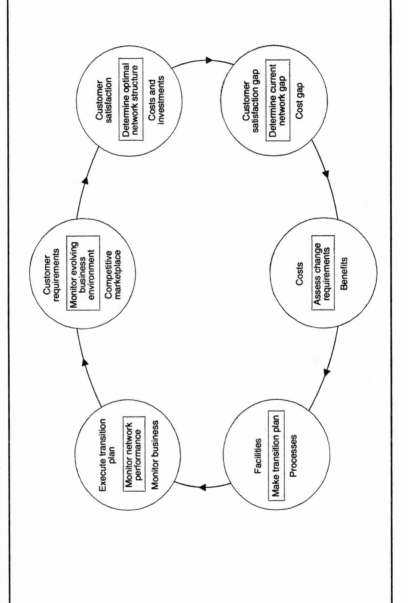

ments, and nearly all the business performance measures available to the business. Figure 4.10 shows the inputs companies usually need to carry out the network transition cycle. They are:

- Competitors' operations and strategies.
- Marketplace environment.
- Marketing strategies.
- Customer requirements.
- Operating costs.
- Manufacturing capacity.
- Customer satisfaction performance.
- Network performance.
- Facilities cost results.
- Product line changes.
- Transportation service environment.
- Regional economics.
- Supplier performance.
- Inventory policies.
- Working capital requirements.
- Cost of capital projections.
- Organization changes.

The Evolving Business Environment

In Chapter 1 we noted a number of forces that companies must monitor to remain competitive and continue to provide acceptable customer satisfaction. Among these were:

- Shorter and overlapping product life cycles.
- Increasing customer demands for service and quality.
- Advances in technology for managing and operating integrated networks.
- Globalization of marketplaces.

These forces, together with a number of other factors in a company's business environment, can have a significant effect on the ability of the

FIGURE 4–10
Inputs Required to Carry Out the Network Transition Cycle

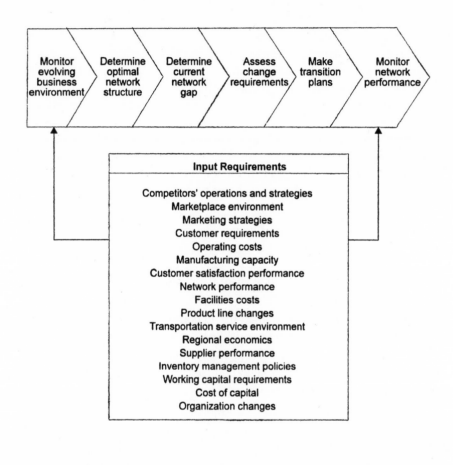

| Monitor evolving business environment | Determine optimal network structure | Determine current network gap | Assess change requirements | Make transition plans | Monitor network performance |

Input Requirements

Competitors' operations and strategies
Marketplace environment
Marketing strategies
Customer requirements
Operating costs
Manufacturing capacity
Customer satisfaction performance
Network performance
Facilities costs
Product line changes
Transportation service environment
Regional economics
Supplier performance
Inventory management policies
Working capital requirements
Cost of capital
Organization changes

integrated network to continue providing customer satisfaction at the lowest possible operating cost and investment. Such other factors include customer desires, geographical shifts in customer locations, raw materials sourcing and cost trends, manufacturing and transportation cost trends, the cost of capital (both equity and debt), and competitors' actions and strategies.

The company's reactions to these forces must be focused on the performance of the integrated network. In particular, the impact of these driving forces must be translated into network performance requirements. So monitoring the evolving business environment means making the connections between business environmental reality and network capabilities. It also requires some projection of current environmental factors into the future, because it may take time to implement some changes. Some possible ways to monitor the business environment and reflect the situation on the network's performance are illustrated in Figure 4.11.

Using the model of a funnel, environmental forces are monitored with fundamental business processes, and their impact is measured with fundamental network performance measures at each type of integrated manufacturing and distribution location. Most companies group the environmental forces they consider to be critical success factors in four groups. These groups are shown at the top of the funnel in Figure 4.11, and their typical contents are:

The Competitive Market Place

- The *products* in the market, including both equivalent products and substitute products, that share the market in each of the segments in which the company may compete.
- The *demand* in the market for all competing products and the rate of total market growth or decline.
- The *competition* for product sales to customers in each market segment, made up of other companies, including competing companies selling substitute products.
- *Customer requirements* for product performance, product quality, product delivery, and all the services customers require of competitors to satisfy their business needs and influence their buying decisions.

Political and Economic Forces

- *Regulations,* which affect product design, entrance to marketing and sales channels, pricing, and other aspects of the product's manufacturing, marketing, distribution, and quality.
- *Country conditions,* which affect how the company may have to alter its business processes to comply with marketplace, political,

FIGURE 4–11
Monitoring the Impact of the Business Environment

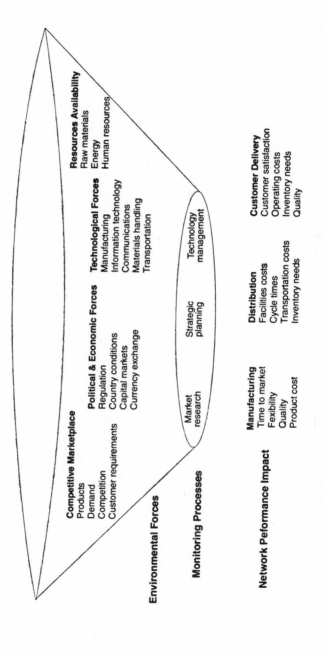

Environmental Forces

Competitive Marketplace
Products
Demand
Competition
Customer requirements

Political & Economic Forces
Regulation
Country conditions
Capital markets
Currency exchange

Technological Forces
Manufacturing
Information technology
Communications
Materials handling
Transportation

Resources Availability
Raw materials
Energy
Human resources

Monitoring Processes

Market research

Strategic planning

Technology management

Network Peformance Impact

Manufacturing
Time to market
Fexibility
Quality
Product cost

Distribution
Facilities costs
Cycle times
Transportation costs
Inventory needs

Customer Delivery
Customer satisfaction
Operating costs
Inventory needs
Quality

89

regulatory, or customer requirements in each of the countries in which the company operates.

• *Capital markets,* whose capacity for equity or debt financing may affect the company's ability to grow, expand, invest in assets, or obtain working capital for operations or inventories.

• *Currency exchange* rates or limitations, which may affect operating or profit margins in different countries or affect the access to revenues and profits a company may wish to move from one currency to another to minimize the exchange rate risk over time.

Technology Forces

• *Manufacturing technology,* which will affect product quality, cost, and resource needs for production and which could influence decisions about where to manufacture, number of plants, and capacities of plants.

• *Information technology,* whose evolving capabilities could enable more profitable or more effective business processes throughout the company and which could affect access to markets, customer satisfaction, and cycle times throughout the business.

• *Communications* technology, which will affect business operations, cycle times, customer order and delivery processes, and the overall ability of the business to execute its day-to-day business.

• *Materials handling* technology, which will influence decisions about product design, packaging, or labeling, shipping and storage locations and equipment, and quality and cycle times for warehouse, delivery, installation, and post-sales service processes

• *Transportation* technology and efficiency, which may influence decisions about mode or frequency of product shipment, the types of carriers or vehicles used, the quantities transported, or their condition.

Resources Availability

• *Raw materials* supply conditions, which may affect the company's timely access to raw materials as well as the price, quality, and acquisition lead times of those materials.

- *Energy* availability and price, which could affect the company's production, distribution, transportation, and product costs.

- *Human resources* availability in terms of number and location of people and skill sets needed by the company, which could influence the company's time to market, its ability to implement change or new technology, and the quality of its business processes.

Monitoring all of these environmental forces is a complex task. It takes the most skillful resources in the company to gather and maintain knowledge about the environment and make projections into the future to allow for planning beyond the current year. In addition, much of this information is needed by every department or business process in the company, not just integrated network management or design. Therefore, the processes for monitoring the environment are the fundamental business processes most companies employ when external information must be collected and analyzed and effects predicted. The integrated network design process usually expects three business processes to be its monitoring arm and perform much of the analysis needed to translate environmental forces into business impacts that have meaning for network design. Those monitoring processes, shown in the middle of Figure 4.11, are:

- *Market research*—The process that gathers information and analyzes the impact of forces in the competitive marketplace.

- *Strategic planning*—The process usually charged with monitoring and analyzing political and economic forces, resource availability, and some of the competitive marketplace forces.

- *Technology management*—The process that focuses on the evolution of technologies employed in the business and provides direction as to which technologies constitute core competencies for the company, those that help define the company's competitive strengths.

The integrated network design process has the ongoing responsibility of keeping these three monitoring processes completely informed about what forces will have an impact on the network's performance. As a result, market research, strategic planning, and technology management know where to focus their efforts, and have the insight to help translate changing environmental conditions into network impacts.

However, the manufacturing, distribution, and customer delivery processes have the final responsibility for translating business environmental forces into network performance. Their responsibilities usually lead them to measure environmental forces in the following ways:

Manufacturing

- Time to market.
- Flexibility.
- Quality.
- Product cost.

Distribution

- Facilities costs.
- Transportation costs.
- Cycle time.
- Inventory needs.

Customer Delivery

- Customer satisfaction.
- Operating costs.
- Inventory needs.
- Quality.

The Optimal Network Design

The optimal network is that configuration of network locations, facilities, and business policies that yields the network's fundamental objective: *customer satisfaction at the lowest possible cost and investment*. Certainly every company would like to have an optimal network. But we know from long experience that once achieved, this is a goal that few companies can sustain for long. This is because both the external business environment, which we discussed above, and the internal operating environment of the company are dynamic and sometimes unpredictable. An optimal network, designed and implemented at a given time, may quickly lose its effectiveness as one or more of its design criteria change.

In addition, few companies can make changes in their network rapidly enough to remain optimal in dynamic and perhaps uncertain marketplaces. Network changes can involve facilities changes or relocations, capacity expansion, or the introduction of new policies or business rules. These changes usually take months or years to implement. The cost of change is usually high, forcing most companies to be quite careful and highly circumspect about network changes.

Nevertheless, there is significant value in determining what an optimal network would look like. Company management can use the information for such purposes as:

- Understanding how different the existing network is from an optimal network.
- Evaluating the potential cost, revenue, and profit implications of this difference.
- Adding insight to the criteria on which optimality is based.
- Planning the time frame and extent of network changes required to obtain or move closer to an optimal network.

Defining the optimal network entails answering the following questions:

- What is the planning horizon needed for network evaluation and possible change?
- What customer requirements must be met?
- What products in what volumes will customers demand over the desired planning horizon, and year by year during the planning horizon?
- What levels of service in each customer segment will be required to achieve the desired level of customer satisfaction?
- What manufacturing capacity will be needed?
- What pattern of manufacturing or production output will provide the manufacturing capacity assumed?
- How many plants will there be, where will the plants be located, and which products will they make?
- How many distribution centers will there be and where should they be located?
- What products in what volumes will each distribution center handle?

- Which distribution centers will serve each customer delivery location and the customers it serves?

- What transportation capacities, modes, and frequency will be required to serve the total flow of product in the network?

- What will be the lowest possible operating and investment costs for achieving customer satisfaction with all of the above network characteristics?

The opportunity to define the optimal network will also satisfy several other planning needs of the company. These might include manufacturing operations issues such as supplier sources, financial projections for network operation and management, and marketing strategies for customer profitability or product profitability.

A discussion of the methods available to company management for designing an optimal network can be found in Chapter 7 in the section entitled, Decision Support—Modeling Systems.

LESSONS FOR MANAGERS

An integrated manufacturing and distribution network is a daunting business environment. The network consists of nearly all the company's operational assets. Most, if not all, of the company's people work somewhere in the integrated network. Costs incurred in the network are large and have a significant impact on the company's profit. How can managers get their arms around such a challenging business process and actually understand how network design and operations influence customer satisfaction?

We think that the most promising approach is to take a business process view of the integrated network, as we have done in this book. The network functions as a set of interconnected business processes. Figure 4.3 provides a good illustration of the interconnected processes. In Figure 4.3 we can see how three important processes work together to satisfy customer needs.

The three processes are production, supply, and order management. They span the traditional organization, which had separate departments for manufacturing, distribution, and customer delivery.

The process view opens up a wealth of performance improvement opportunities for network managers. Business process improvement can address both the tactical and the strategic improvements we called for in network design and operation. It also allows managers to take a process-oriented approach to performance measurement, which we illustrate in Chapter 6.

CHAPTER 5

INVENTORY MANAGEMENT

In the integrated manufacturing and distribution network, inventory management is the process of deploying and moving raw materials, work-in-process, and finished products through the network to satisfy customer requirements. The inventory management process is applied across the entire integrated network to manage the flow of materials to, between, and through every type of location—manufacturing, distribution, and customer delivery. The performance of the inventory management process is measured by the total amount of inventory, or its working capital equivalent, needed to achieve the company's customer satisfaction goals. Elements of customer satisfaction usually affected by the inventory management process include:

- *Customer service levels*—The probability that products will be available from inventories, in their expected locations, to satisfy customer demand—measured in service level percent or its inverse, stockout percent.

- *Customer delivery quality*—The ability to deliver products from inventories to customers at the agreed time, in a complete and accurate order—measured by on-time delivery and order completeness and accuracy.

- *Customer delivery cycle time*—The time required to fill an order from the appropriate inventory location—measured in cycle time duration or variance from target.

Most companies set a goal of satisfying customer requirements with the lowest amount of inventory possible and constantly seek ways to reduce inventory investment requirements.

FIGURE 5–1
Possible Inventory Locations

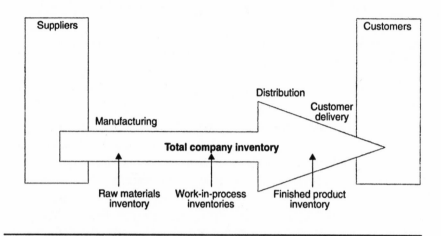

In this chapter we will explore the types of inventory in the network and their roles and value. We will then describe effective strategic and tactical inventory planning processes that allow companies to achieve acceptable customer satisfaction.

WHAT IS INVENTORY?

Inventory is the total set of materials found in the integrated manufacturing and distribution network that are used to achieve customer satisfaction. The form of inventory changes as materials move through the network. Inventories range from *raw materials* to *work in process* to *finished goods*. As shown in Figure 5.1, inventory locations can be found throughout the integrated network in manufacturing, distribution, and customer delivery locations. We can also have inventory outside the company's traditional network. We can speak of inventory at the company's suppliers, inventory owned by suppliers and placed at company locations, and inventory at customers' locations. We see inventory either at rest or in motion. Inventory also has the dimension of time associated with it when we speak of just-in-time (JIT) production or just-in-time delivery. Time also is a dimension when we use the term *inventory position* to capture inventories both on-hand and on-order (or in transit).

The value of inventory can best be seen in the context of the entire integrated manufacturing and distribution network. When we look at the entire network, as in Figure 5.1, we can see the totality of inventory in whatever form it may take throughout the network. We also avoid seeing inventory as simply materials that separate or buffer one location in the network from another. This older, traditional role of inventory is fast becoming obsolete. Inventories that buffer one location from another have become obsolete because they contribute to higher but avoidable costs, they slow down the flow of products to customers, and they mask other conditions, such as inefficient order management and unbalanced capacities among locations in the network, that ought to be avoided.

In this context we look at inventory management as a process that takes place across the entire network. This is the best way to consider inventory management, because it allows us to focus on the role and value of inventory in the network rather than at any individual location. Inventory management activities that do take place at individual locations will be considered for their contribution to overall integrated manufacturing and distribution performance, especially in the role each location plays in customer satisfaction.

CONCEPTS THAT GUIDE INVENTORY MANAGEMENT

In the integrated network there are three important concepts we will follow in describing the inventory management process:

- There is just one total inventory in the company and in the integrated manufacturing and distribution network.
- Good information about customer requirements and product demand and raw materials supply is the best substitute available for inventory.
- The inventory management process is the management of the *flow* of materials in the network, not the management of stocks at each location in the network.

One Inventory in the Network

Rather than speak separately of inventories for manufacturing, distribution, and customer delivery, we prefer to view all materials used to satisfy customers as a single inventory. Then the inventory management process has the critical responsibility for allocating working capital among inventories that, at any given moment, happen to be in one location or another, or one form or another. We can also better understand the process of adding value to materials as they flow through the network and change their form from raw materials to work in process and ultimately to finished goods. This value-adding process, the focus of which must always be customer satisfaction, explains how best to manage the actual or implicit allocations companies make among the various forms of inventory.

Substituting Information for Inventory

Most companies come to understand that all inventories are their last resort in dealing with uncertainties. Raw materials inventories represent manufacturing difficulty in predicting production requirements and quantities or the availability of supply. Distribution and customer delivery inventories are ways to deal with customer demand uncertainty. More and better information reduces uncertainty. Less uncertainty means less inventory. Investing in inventories has become a poor substitute for gaining and communicating better information about customer requirements and customer demand throughout the integrated network.

Managing the Flow of Inventory

The inventory management process has the same goal as all other business processes we have spoken of—achieve customer satisfaction at the lowest possible cost and investment. Companies satisfy customers through the timely delivery of products. To get products to customers, materials must flow through the network efficiently and value must be added throughout the flow. Managing inventories means managing the flow of materials throughout the network. Seeing inventory management in this context yields better performance measures for inventories and for the entire network. Since all network locations are involved in the flow of materials toward customers, they share equally in the same customer satisfaction goals. No location can be isolated by an inventory of materials that excludes the location's performance when seen in the light of customer satisfaction.

To show how these concepts yield effective inventory management performance, we will first describe the forms of inventory in the integrated manufacturing and distribution network, then discuss the use and value of inventory throughout the network, and finally describe the operation of the inventory management process in the network.

ONE INVENTORY IN THE INTEGRATED NETWORK

By one inventory in the integrated network, we mean the sum of all the materials at all locations in the network, in whatever form the inventory happens to be at that time. This is a conceptual view of the inventory. We understand that at any time we can go to every location in the network and see each individual inventory and the inventory in transit between locations. This is the physical view of the inventory. However, a physical view does not tell us very much about each inventory's role in satisfying customers.

Raw materials inventories, should there be any in manufacturing, are not in a form that will satisfy customers. They have a long way to go before we can see value in them from a customer's point of view. Finished goods inventories at distribution locations are in a form that will satisfy customers, but they may not be in the right place. Only the total inventory tells us where the network stands relative to satisfying customers.

Time—the cycle time to satisfy customers—is another inventory dimension to consider. Some inventory, usually finished goods already located at customer delivery locations, is immediately ready to satisfy customers. Other inventory in the network will be ready only in the future, say when manufacturing or distribution flows are completed. Only the total network inventory and its flow toward customers provide a view of the company's ability to satisfy customers over time.

It is the dynamic flow of materials through the network that has meaning in the context of customer satisfaction. The order management process, discussed in Chapter 3, pulls materials through the network in response to customer orders. The flow this creates is the focus of the inventory management process. For this reason we find it much more effective for companies to focus on the entire inventory as it flows through the network.

The traditional alternative has been to focus on inventories in individual locations, one at a time, looking at their sizes and turnovers and the service levels they provided only to the places each location served, rather than customer order service. In this mode, locations upstream from customer delivery locations, such as manufacturing and distribution locations, could never see the impact they had on customer satisfaction. That situation clearly is no longer desirable. Nowadays, companies want to see the customer satisfaction impact of each location. Companies need to measure the performance of the entire network, because most of their decisions revolve around creating and managing the integrated network to achieve customer satisfaction goals.

Raw Materials Inventories

Raw materials are the original materials, parts, components, or supplies used in the manufacturing process. They are used to create or assemble finished products. They are added to the product, along with labor, to increase value as the production process is carried out. They can be purchased from other companies or supplied by other plants in the integrated network. Every production process must have on hand inventories of its component parts or materials to function, though they could be very small as in just-in-time inventories. The size of those inventories depends on a broad range of factors, including supply source lead times, production rates or batch sizes, the uncertainty of supply, and the uncertainty of production schedules or customer demand, whichever drives the plant's activities.

Another important factor that determines inventory sizes or levels is the inventory planning and replenishment process used to decide when to order and how much to order when supplying production processes or replenishing raw materials inventories. Inventory planning and replenishment are two separate steps. Inventory planning in a manufacturing environment revolves around determining demand for raw materials. Inventory replenishment revolves around traditional inventory concerns, such as supplier delivery times; quantity concerns, such as minimums and transportation costs; and vendor supply capacities and service quality.

Nearly all manufacturing locations have adopted an inventory planning practice in which raw materials demand is derived from actual production schedules. Using MRP (materials requirements planning or manufacturing resource planning) manufacturers create a future production schedule called a master schedule. Exploding the master schedule down to the components level will determine the precise raw materials requirements at each point on the scheduling horizon. These requirements can be compared to the raw materials inventory position at corresponding points, providing the best estimate or a forecast of raw materials demand.

What has changed drastically during recent years is the way in which manufacturers replenish raw materials inventories in response to their demand forecasts. Rather than use traditional replenishment practices based on order points and order quantities and variations of the economic lot size (EOQ) formula, manufacturers are progressively moving to a just-in-time inventory replenishment policy. The elements of just-in-time inventory in the manufacturing environment are:

- Close working relations with suppliers so that delivery lead times and order sizes can be as small as possible, tied as closely as possible to exact daily production requirements for raw materials.

- Delivery of raw materials directly to the production floor, bypassing receiving and storage activities.

- High flexibility in production activities so that schedules, and therefore raw materials needs, are no longer tied to long, fixed production schedules for a mix of products.

- Rapid changeover capabilities in every production center so that batch sizes are small and production rates can be changed rapidly.

The impact of this practice is significantly reduced raw materials inventory needs and increased manufacturing flexibility for the product mix. The overall impact in the integrated network is even more striking. With manufacturing operating in a much more flexible environment, manufacturing lead times are much shorter, thereby reducing finished goods inventories in the network.

Even more raw materials inventory changes are evolving today. To reduce time and costs further, many manufacturers have made agreements with their vendors to take over the raw materials supply process completely. Vendors are given the freedom to stock their manufacturing customer's production line. Manufacturers pay for what they use in the production run rather than for what they ordered or received. Vendors have complete

information about production schedules and provide raw materials accordingly. Numerous costs and cycle times are removed from the raw materials
supply process for both vendor and manufacturer. Among the activities that
can be eliminated or minimized are purchasing, inventory status monitoring,
receiving, storage, picking, inspection, and accounts payable. This makes
good sense for many manufacturers and certainly contributes to their
competitive capabilities.

Work-in-Process Inventories

Work-in-process, or WIP, inventories are intermediate work products of
the manufacturing process. They range from assemblies of parts with a
low value added to near-ready finished products awaiting final touches
such as customization for specific customer orders. For accounting
reasons, some companies consider everything in the plant as WIP. WIP
exists because of the design of the product and the design of the manufacturing process. Other reasons for WIP involve the manufacturing
cycle time. To reduce cycle time, say from order to delivery, many
companies maintain WIP. They invest value in the product in advance
of demand so that when that demand is realized, they can satisfy it in
relatively short order.

As manufacturing processes become faster and more flexible, the need
for WIP is reduced accordingly. Most companies are seeking to re-engineer
their manufacturing processes so they can achieve make-to-customer-or-
der. They no longer require their plants to produce at steady rates when
customer demand may not be at all steady. In addition, by finding ways to
produce products in smaller quantities, the WIP that accumulates because
of previously efficient "economic production runs" is smaller. This has
been applied to both discrete flow and continuous flow manufacturing
processes. WIP still remains a relatively fixed feature of bulk processes
where production quantities are more a function of the size and scale of
manufacturing facilities (a chemical reactor vessel, for example) than of
customer order patterns.

Some WIP can be found at locations other than manufacturing. For
many products, the last steps in configuring or customizing the product
for a particular customer order can be performed at a distribution or
customer delivery location. The final assembly of personal computers
has this characteristic in many companies. PCs are positioned in distri-

bution locations where, according to customer order, tailored configurations of software and hardware are made. Indeed, most of the PC industry now postpones final assembly until customer orders are in hand. So in many companies, WIP extends throughout the integrated network.

Finished Goods Inventories

Finished goods inventories are stocks of products that are ready to serve customers. Their value to customers, however, depends on their location and the readiness of the company to combine the product with the services necessary to satisfy customers. This typically occurs at customer delivery facilities. Finished inventories exist to meet customer requirements, which go far beyond just the product itself. Therefore finished goods inventories must be positioned and maintained to meet customer requirements for:

- The right quantity and product mix.
- The right timeliness of delivery.
- The right combination of product delivery time and the timing of all the associated services that customer orders call for, including installation, delivery services, and product support (training, installation, demonstration, and staging).

The Total Inventory

So companies now focus on the entire inventory. This idea causes them to consider the inventory management process in the following light:

- Seeing their inventory as just one inventory allows companies to focus on making just one *inventory plan* for the ongoing deployment of total inventory or its working capital equivalent.
- Having all network locations and operations agree on, and execute, one inventory plan provides the connection to customer satisfaction that all locations and operations need.
- Making just one inventory plan results in lower total working capital requirements and lower total network operating costs to achieve a desired level of customer satisfaction.

Let us consider what has led companies to these conclusions over the last several years.

Separate versus Collective Inventory Planning

Recall that the goal of the integrated network is customer satisfaction at the lowest possible cost and investment. A significant part of investment, sometimes more than half of all working capital used in the business, is inventory. Planning the investment of working capital was traditionally a highly decentralized process. It was divided among manufacturing and distribution (or marketing) units. Each unit might have used different and sometimes conflicting performance goals that were not focused entirely on customer satisfaction.

For example, in the past, manufacturing focused exclusively on efficiency and cost. Those goals could lead to raw materials inventory planning and investment levels that offered manufacturing efficiency but hindered manufacturing flexibility—the ability to respond to changing customer order patterns. Manufacturing flexibility can have a positive effect on customer satisfaction. But manufacturers wanted to minimize raw material inventories independent of other factors in the business. Costs might have been lower, but flexibility was low as well. Customer satisfaction was not a goal in any real sense. With minimal raw materials inventories, manufacturing could not respond rapidly to changes in the market, because they had to wait for raw materials inventories to grow, and they were at the mercy of their raw materials supply lead times.

In response to this inflexible manufacturing environment, distribution units, whose goals were oriented to customer satisfaction, planned finished inventories that were large enough to allow for the inflexibility of manufacturing. These inventories were planned and deployed as if manufacturing were in a different world or, at the very least, a different company. Large distribution inventories offered customer satisfaction but at a high cost. In many companies, the basis of finished inventories growth was the internal relationship between manufacturing and distribution rather than customer satisfaction or market growth.

Manufacturing and distribution units made their plans independently of one another. The results were costly and offered little opportunity to achieve better customer satisfaction. As a result many companies came to understand that planning manufacturing and distribution inventories separately was unproductive. The practice led to higher total inventory invest-ments and did nothing to improve the company's ability to satisfy custom-ers. Having realized this, companies have begun to seek a better approach to inventory planning and deployment.

A Better Approach

A better approach is to have all network locations collectively plan and deploy inventories using customer satisfaction as the single goal of the entire integrated manufacturing and distribution network. This provides the needed connection to customer satisfaction by allowing the company to evaluate the role and value of all inventories simultaneously. It also serves to break down the sometimes unproductive and artificial barriers between manufacturing and distribution by giving them a common set of customer satisfaction goals.

The context that all network locations use for this simultaneous plan-ning must take into account the following factors:

- *The company's marketing strategies*—Those competitive strate-gies that guide the customer delivery objectives of the company, that is the company's time to deliver a customer order and assure that the total delivery meets customer requirements for complete-ness and quality.

- *The company's manufacturing strategies*—The manner in which products are manufactured, taking into account the costs of manu-facturing, which give rise to such characteristics as production lot sizes, time to produce products from raw materials, raw materials acquisition lead times, and the time to change from manufacturing one product to another when products share manufacturing capac-ity or facilities.

- *The integrated network's cycle times*—The amount of time needed to transport product from one location to another using available transportation modes and the time each location needs to make ready a shipment.

- *The cost structure of the business*—The relative costs of materials, labor, transportation, customer delivery services, and the general and administrative expenses throughout the integrated network.

• *The patterns of customer demand*—The levels and variation in product demand for each of the products that the company sells and the predictability of this demand over both short and long periods.

INVENTORY PLANNING PROCESSES

The process of inventory planning for most companies is a continuous process made up of two ongoing efforts:

• *Tactical inventory planning*—Inventory planning that seeks to optimize customer satisfaction within the design and constraints of the existing integrated network.
• *Strategic inventory planning*—Inventory planning that seeks to optimize customer satisfaction through changes in any or all components of the integrated network, including manufacturing processes, distribution and customer delivery locations, and product flow management processes, rules, and policies.

The success of *tactical inventory planning* is usually measured by assessing customer satisfaction on a day-to-day basis with each customer and for all products, considered individually and collectively. Customer contact is frequent, as is the measurement of order management performance. The planning recognizes that the capabilities and performance ranges of the integrated network are constant. The plans must reflect the current practicalities of using the network to satisfy customers. That is, manufacturing and distribution patterns are relatively fixed and inflexible. They must also necessarily reflect the total amount of working capital available for inventories throughout the network.

The success of *strategic inventory planning* is usually measured in terms of long-term (one or more years) customer satisfaction and return on investment relative to what competitors can achieve. Strategic inventory planning is allowed much more freedom in its scope and the changes it may suggest for other company strategies, such as marketing, product selection and design, and manufacturing. The entire integrated network's capabilities, capacity, and design are open to question and improvement. The fundamental goal of the integrated network—*to optimize customer satisfaction at the lowest possible cost and investment*—is the central issue in strategic inventory planning. The result of strategic inventory planning is a change in the integrated network, the manufacturing process, and the degree of flexibility available.

To better understand these inventory planning processes, consider the process illustrated in Figure 5.2. We see the two inventory planning processes depicted as concentric circles. Tactical inventory planning is on the inside circle. Strategic inventory planning is on the outside circle. Central to both inventory planning processes is a core of information needed and shared by both. This information consists of:

- Customer requirements.
- Sales forecasts.
- Network performance.
- Network costs.

Let's look at this information first and then consider each of the inventory planning processes that uses the information.

INVENTORY PLANNING INFORMATION NEEDS

Both strategic and tactical inventory planning use the same four types of information in making plans and evaluating their prospective results. While they use the same types of information, each inventory planning process calls for a different view or interpretation of the information and different version of the information. In general, tactical inventory planning uses very detailed versions of the information to focus on short time periods—days, weeks, and months—and on individual products and customers. Strategic inventory planning uses aggregated and summary versions of the same information. The time horizons the information covers will differ, because the time horizon for strategic inventory planning is much longer than that for tactical inventory planning.

The overall use of the four types of information is quite similar. Figure 5.3 illustrates the role of each type of information in our two inventory planning processes. The information sources at the center of the figure are used in both planning processes; tactical inventory plan-

110

FIGURE 5–2
Integrated Inventory Planning

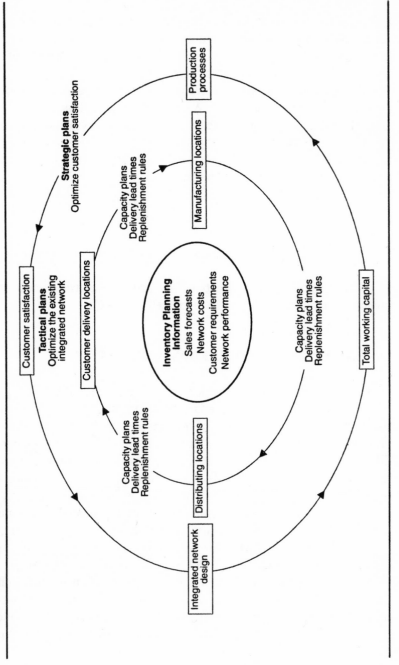

FIGURE 5–3
Information Needs for Inventory Planning

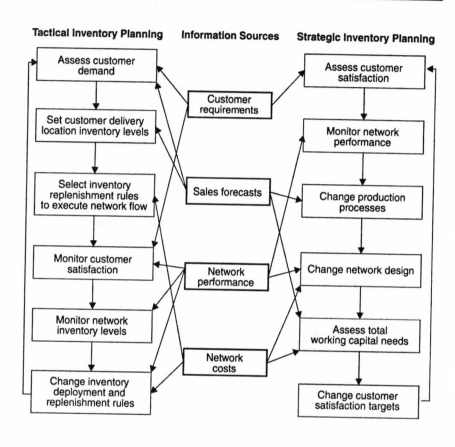

ning is shown at the left, and strategic inventory planning is shown at the right.

Customer Requirements Information

Customer requirements information consists of a broad range of information concerning how products should be made available and delivered to each customer. In its most detailed form, this information must reflect each customer's or class of customers' requirements for each product or group of products when such classes or groups share common characteristics. In an aggregate form, the information should be the total range of requirements that accurately reflects all customers' requirements. Care must be taken to ensure that aggregate information does not obscure the details or the range of requirements. For example, averages may be a poor aggregate measure of customer requirements, because there are few average customers.

Typical elements of customer requirements information are:

Product Requirements Information

- Specific individual product needs.
- Families of products required in concert.
- Product version or configuration standards or exceptions.
- Product quality or yield standards for as-delivered products.

Product Cost Information

- Pricing options for individual products and families of products.
- Contract or agreement terms for product pricing.
- Additional cost inclusions for distribution services, freight, insurance, packaging, and labeling.

Product Ordering Information

- Product availability requirements.
- Customer order volume and product mix specifications.
- Order minimums for individual products and families of products.
- Customer order placement modes.
- Customer order communication channels.
- Order completeness specifications.
- Ordering frequency specifications.
- Backorder options.

Product Delivery Information

• Order delivery lead time or cycle time.
• Delivery frequency options.
• Order completeness requirements or split order options.
• Customer receiving requirements or customer pick-up options.
• Customer returns options.
• Delivery quality requirements.
• Customer routing requirements.

Sales Forecast Information

Inventories exist for several reasons. Some are created to gain cost economies, such as production and transportation efficiencies. Economic lot sizes in production environments or in multi-echelon replenishment are good examples. These are implemented to achieve the lowest total cost when both fixed and variable costs must be balanced in operations. Lower transportation costs for full truckload quantities are another reason. More inventory than needed for customer satisfaction is accumulated or transported to achieve a lower unit transportation cost. The same balancing of fixed and variable costs is inherent in full truckload transportation, because full truckload freight rates usually yield lower unit transportation costs.

Inventories also exist because there remains significant uncertainty in every company's business. Try as we might to eliminate uncertainty, we have yet to succeed. Uncertainty exists in the timing, quantity, and location of customer demand. Similarly, there is uncertainty in what raw materials will be needed to satisfy that customer demand. Inventories help companies manage uncertainty and ensure that they can offer customer satisfaction at the level of performance they believe is required and competitive.

Over longer periods, other types of uncertainty must be managed as well. In considering planning horizons of more than one year, and perhaps extending to five or more years, uncertainty exists in such critical business factors as the overall market size for a product, the company's market share, the potential life of the product, and substitutes for a product, plus shifts in the way the company might do business. Business shifts might involve expansion or contraction of country market coverage or a choice of whether to participate in a product's entire integrated network or just parts of it. For example, a company may shift from selling to independent distributors to selling to end customers or consumers directly. Other factors influencing product sales include questions of technology and regulation that come from sources beyond a company's control.

Where there is uncertainty, whether short-term or long-term, companies must make predictions—must decide today what the company will do in the future. Sales forecasts are such predictions. They are decisions made today to plan the future. Forecasts do not minimize or eliminate uncertainty, but they allow actions to be taken under the company's lowest cost prediction of the future.

In the integrated network there is good reason to have one and only one sales forecast rather than separate and independent forecasts prepared by the components of the network—manufacturing, distribution, and customer delivery. Manufacturing ought to be making what distribution and customer delivery are planning to deliver. Likewise, customer delivery would not be able to satisfy customers if manufacturing were not acquiring the raw materials for those products. This concept can be extended to all the other processes in the company, including sales, marketing, and finance. Most companies forecast capital requirements, personnel needs, cash flow, costs, and prices. Most, if not all of these forecasts should be based on the same set of fundamental predictions of sales that the integrated network uses.

Typical elements of sales forecast information include:

- Historical sales.
- Competitors' sales.
- Total market sales.
- Total market demand.
- Historical forecast accuracy.
- Product life cycle stages—new, mature, or declining.
- Product development plans or planned changes.
- Promotion plans.
- Pricing plans.
- Competitors' strategies for equivalent products, substitute products, and product replacements.
- Economic trends affecting customer demand.
- Technological trends affecting demand.

- Short-term product availability.
- Long-term product availability or raw materials availability.
- Sales force and sales management predictions.
- New markets or markets that may not be available due to geographical considerations.

Network Performance Information

While sales forecast information helps the company manage inventories under the uncertainty that arises from external sources—principally in the marketplace—network performance information helps the company manage uncertainty that arises from sources internal to the network. Internal uncertainties arise from two sources:

- The time factors for network operations.
- The accuracy of network operations.

The inventory needed to satisfy customers is dependent on the time needed to replenish each location in the network from its replenishment source. Basic inventory management recognizes that as replenishment lead times get longer, inventory requirements to provide the same level of customer satisfaction get larger. It also recognizes that as the variability of lead times increases (variability being a measure of uncertainty) inventory levels must be larger to provide an equivalent assurance of customer satisfaction.

Accuracy of network operations has a similar impact on inventory needs at each location. Accuracy includes order contents and quantity accuracy, order completeness, and inventory records accuracy.

Network performance information is applicable to tactical inventory planning, because uncertainties in day-to-day delivery time factors and order accuracy can be translated directly into inventory levels needed to assure customer satisfaction. Their impact on strategic inventory planning is less critical, primarily because such uncertainties are replaced by network design criteria to reduce the uncertainty.

The network performance information related to time uncertainty that is needed for inventory planning is:

- *Order filling cycle time*—The time each location needs to bring an order to readiness for shipping; the time elements involved include obtaining or capturing the order information, dispatching the order for location and picking, move times within the network facility, packaging and labeling if necessary, recording the selection and moves, and waiting until the order can be loaded on a transportation vehicle.Inherent in some measures of order filling time is whether the order can be filled completely on the first attempt or whether it must wait for portions of the order to be filled at a later time, giving rise to a split order.

- *Transportation cycle time*—The time needed to ship product from one location to another using each of the transportation modes planned for the network—air, sea, truck, and rail.

- *Order receiving cycle time*—The time needed to process an order upon its receipt at an inventory location, encompassing the time required to unload the order, identify it, record its availability for filling orders at the receiving location, and store the products in the proper locations in the facility.

The network performance information related to accuracy uncertainty that is needed for inventory planning is:

- *Order contents and quantities*—Do the order contents accurately reflect what was ordered and the quantities ordered?

- *Order completeness*—Do orders arrive in one complete shipment, or are they split among several shipments which arrive at unpredictable times?

- *Inventory records accuracy*—Does the information concerning inventory balances and locations accurately reflect the physical quantities and locations of inventory in each location?

NETWORK COST INFORMATION

Inventory planning is one of the ways in which companies can make trade-offs between fixed and variable costs or between investments and operating costs. We saw in Chapter 4 that network costs consist of operating costs and investments. In the context of inventory planning, these costs and investments depend on decisions about where to hold inventory and how much inventory to hold. The reverse is true as well; inventory planning decisions, both strategic and tactical, depend on the cost structure of the integrated network.

The cost structure of the integrated network includes manufacturing, distribution, and customer delivery location costs as well as the transportation costs involved in moving product between locations. In strategic inventory planning, the first issue to consider is the cost of manufacturing. In manufacturing, with costs based on capacity and flexibility, manufacturing cycle time is a key predictor of inventory requirements downstream in the integrated network. Shorter cycles, or shorter manufacturing lead times, mean less finished inventory needed in the integrated network. Care must be taken, however, to evaluate the amount of work-in-process and raw materials inventories needed to allow for shorter cycle times.

Other strategic inventory issues revolve around numbers of distribution and customer delivery locations. These numbers determine the amount of inventory in the network at any one time. Inventory capital requirements are a function of 'he amount of inventory needed to support the current or prospective number of inventory stocking locations. Operating costs and performance at each location are also elements of inventory holding cost.

The network cost information needed for both tactical and strategic inventory planning includes:

- *Product cost*—The cost of each product at each location in the network, considering the value added as the product moves from manufacturing to customer.

- *Transportation cost*—Costs incurred throughout the network for moving product between locations and to customers.

- *Inventory holding cost*—A measure of the total cost incurred for holding inventory over time, made up of network costs consisting of storage costs, shrinkage (loss) and damage costs, obsolescence costs, ad valorem costs (taxes and insurance), and capital cost.

- *Inventory operations cost*—Sometimes called ordering cost, consisting of the activity-based costs which accompany the management and administration of inventory flow throughout the network.

FIGURE 5–4
The Strategic Inventory Planning Process

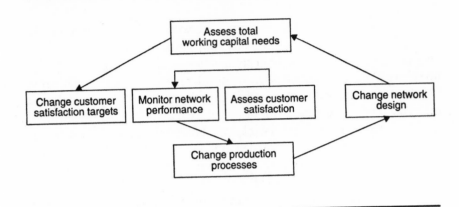

STRATEGIC INVENTORY PLANNING

Strategic inventory planning is inventory planning that seeks to optimize customer satisfaction through changes in any or all components of the integrated network, including manufacturing processes, distribution and customer delivery locations, and product flow management processes, rules, and policies. If we isolate the strategic inventory planning process illustrated in Figure 5.2, we see, in Figure 5.4, that it is centered on customer satisfaction and that the dynamics address strategic changes in the way the company configures its manufacturing, distribution, and customer delivery network, the impact that has on customer satisfaction, and the changes made in the integrated manufacturing and distribution network to set and achieve customer satisfaction targets.

In the strategic context, companies are seeking to optimize customer satisfaction among large groups of targeted customers rather than for individual customers. Tactical inventory planning focuses on satisfying individual customers. Companies' strategic objectives revolve around serving entire market segments and delivering products to satisfy the requirements of each segment in which the company chooses to compete. Strategic inventory planning deals with how to *get to market* over time frames of many years. The planning horizons should be consistent with such company factors as product life cycles, market segment growth patterns, and competitive conditions—the fundamental elements of corporate strategic planning.

While companies may differ in the ways they choose to implement strategic inventory planning, nearly all integrated manufacturing and distribution companies follow a process (as in Figure 5.4) consisting of these six fundamental steps:

- *Assess customer satisfaction*—For each market segment, assess the level of customer satisfaction that has been achieved with current inventory deployment and the allocation of working capital to inventory across the integrated network.

- *Monitor network performance*—Monitor the network performance in terms of capital and operating costs that have been incurred to achieve customer satisfaction with current network inventory flow management policies, rules, and procedures.

- *Change production processes*—When customer satisfaction fails to achieve competitive, profitable levels or in the quest for a leading competitive position, explore alternate production processes whose output is more compatible with customer requirements than current practices.

- *Change network design*—With the same motivations as above, explore network design changes that improve customer satisfaction while improving the return on working capital employed in inventory and network facilities and operations.

- *Assess total working capital needs*— Compare working capital needs for current inventory deployments with those derived from options explored in the proceeding two steps.

- *Change customer satisfaction targets*—Based on these results, plan customer satisfaction levels or targets that the company must achieve to remain competitive or to excel in the market segments in question.

Let's examine ways to carry out each of these strategic inventory steps and the factors and conditions companies consider in their planning.

Strategic Inventory Planning and Customer Satisfaction

The elements of customer satisfaction that are related to inventories in the integrated network are speed of product delivery and quality of customer order performance. For strategic inventory planning, these measures of customer satisfaction are applied to entire market segments in which the company chooses to compete. A market segment is a group of customers for which product and competitor choices are very similar. They are customers whose buying decisions are based on similar needs or patterns. For some products, market segments may divide along lines such as volume of purchases or customer distribution channels. When the buying process makes a difference, companies sometimes segment their market accordingly, as when companies divide government customers from others. Sometimes the only significant segmentation of customers is by their geographical locations—international versus domestic or New England versus the Midwest, Southwest, and West.

The strategic use of inventory then reflects the company's competitive needs in satisfying each market segment's buying and delivery requirements. To capture the essence of these competitive issues, we can focus on the role of inventory in delivery time competition. The strategic inventory planning process begins with an assessment of customer satisfaction.

Customer satisfaction should be assessed against the delivery time requirements found in each market segment. Delivery time satisfaction is usually a function of the availability of product to meet customer orders in a time that customers require. The location and availability of product depend on where in the integrated network the product resides when the order is received. Servicing the orders for an entire market segment calls for strategic deployment of product availability. Companies have many choices in this. One fundamental choice is between the make-to-order and make-to-stock modes of production. Clearly, if customer requirements can be met satisfactorily or competitively directly from production output, inventories are not needed. However, most companies in competitive market segments are highly motivated to improve delivery speed by deploying inventories. They usually must weigh the cost of doing so against the potential loss of sales to speedier competitors.

Once it is decided that make-to-stock is the competitive direction to take, the next step is translating customer requirements into inventory deployment strategies. Such strategies, to serve an entire market segment, revolve around the where-to-stock question and the delivery service quality for each customer served. Delivery time remains the driving force, so inventories deployed throughout the distribution and customer delivery locations must provide the desired delivery time performance.

Each market segment may require its own customer satisfaction assessment. Many companies ultimately have to make strategic trade-offs among market segments if working capital for inventories is limited. While those trade-offs are strategic business decisions, they are usually supported by strategic inventory planning because their impact must be measured in terms of customer satisfaction as well as the potential profitability of each market segment and its relative value to the business in competitive terms.

Strategic Inventory Planning and Network Performance

Companies usually seek to satisfy the needs of many different customer segments through a common manufacturing, distribution, and customer stocking network. The same products, sold into several different customer segments, usually must follow a common network flow due to their common sources for manufacturing and the limited number of distribution and customer delivery locations a company can afford to maintain. As a result, the network's configuration of locations and product holding and shipping capacities is a design compromise for each of the segments served. Network performance must be closely monitored to assure that every customer segment is receiving the service and quality needed to meet its requirements. The network investments and operating costs must also be monitored to provide company management with measures of the return on investment achieved for each customer segment.

The second step in strategic inventory planning is monitoring network performance. The measures of network performance outlined in Chapter 4 should be applied to one customer segment at a time and then in aggregate to assess how the network is serving each customer or market segment. The focus for strategic inventory planning is the impact of network performance on inventory investments across the network. The performance measures are *product investment* measures and network cost factors for serving each market or customer segment.

Most network performance measurement methods make it difficult for companies to separate or allocate network performance measures among different customer or market segments. Network performance is usually reported for so-called functional entities such as distribution centers or inventory accounts. But strategic decisions affecting the way a company serves a particular customer market require performance measurement to be visible by individual customer segment. To obtain these measures, network performance must be broken down among the customer segments supported by common network facilities and investments. To do this, companies should:

- Divide the total customer demand for a product among the different customer or market segments that buy the product.
- Do the same at each inventory stocking location and divide the total product flow into and out of each stocking location according to the same customer segments.
- Apply the network performance measures for each individual segment product flow as if the others did not exist (use an allocation method to divide operating costs, working capital, and investment costs among the product-customer segment flows).
- Monitor the performance and analyze the effectiveness of the network for each product-customer segment.

Strategic Inventory Planning and Production Processes

Production processes are the ways companies choose to operate their plants or factories in terms of the schedule of output and the allocation of time or capacity to the various products produced at their plants or factories. Most production processes provide the basics relating to each product's production plans and schedules, answering such questions as:

- When will the product be made again?
- In what quantities will the product be made?
- In what sequence will each product be made when many products share the same production lines or production equipment?
- How much flexibility will be allowed in these production process characteristics or rules?
- What planning horizon will be used for fixed, unalterable production schedules?
- What is the ordering lead time required to obtain production output when the distribution and customer service locations want more product?

If we have the answers to these questions about the production process and we know how our integrated network is configured, we can immediately understand the implications for inventory needs in the network. Production quantities and the time between production lots will dictate the amount of inventory needed in the network to satisfy customer demand at a given level of service.

Given the production process answers and the network configuration, we can understand the customer service levels the network can achieve; thus we can estimate the impact on customer satisfaction. Should these results yield customer satisfaction that fails to achieve competitive, profitable levels or a leading competitive position, we may conclude that our strategic inventory plans can no longer achieve the desired results. If network configuration changes (the number and location of distribution and customer delivery facilities) do not yield satisfactory improvements in customer satisfaction, we may have to turn to changes in the production processes themselves.

The principal reason for seeking changes in the production process is that inventory availability is well below levels needed to satisfy customers. In the strategic inventory planning context, this means that entire market segments or product lines are failing to achieve satisfactory levels. The types of changes in the production process that are capable of alleviating these kinds of problems include rapid increases in the overall capacity of the factories or plants and major changes in the allocation of production capacity within or among several plants. Either option represents a significant change in manufacturing strategy and production process characteristics.

Strategic Inventory Planning and Network Design

Network design becomes an issue in strategic inventory planning when the number and locations of distribution and customer service facilities are not cost-effective in achieving customer satisfaction for one or more of the company's market segments. When products in this segment are not getting to market effectively and when the working capital for the inventory required to achieve customer satisfaction no longer provides an acceptable return on investment, changes in the network itself become an option for restoring customer satisfaction at the lowest cost possible.

Network changes have significant impact on inventory, because the number of distribution and customer delivery locations determines how much inventory is needed to achieve a desired level of customer satisfaction. Most strategic inventory management policies require more inventory as the number of locations increases, and vice versa. Similarly, the ability to serve a particular market segment with a given investment of working capital in inventory declines as the number of locations increases. Companies face a classic trade-off, one that has been a fundamental characteristic of inventory management for more than 200 years: in serving a market segment, fewer locations yield lower inventory needs, but customer delivery times and overall service suffer. Increasing the number of inventory locations improves customer satisfaction, but total inventories need to be higher.

Assess Total Working Capital Needs

Strategic inventory planning seeks to optimize customer satisfaction in serving individual market segments. However, in every corporate setting constraints are imposed on the limits or value of customer satisfaction. Chief among the constraints is the availability or cost of working capital to finance inventories. So customer satisfaction, achieved through strategic decisions about production processes and network design, has a cost when the resulting inventories are tallied—the cost of the working capital equivalent of the inventory. More inventory requires more working capital, which must be borrowed or allocated from corporate cash flow or retained earnings. In either case, there is a direct cost, usually called the *cost of capital,* which is one of the typical elements of inventory carrying cost.

Assessing inventory working capital needs calls for estimating how changes in production processes, network design, or customer satisfaction targets will affect inventory in the total manufacturing and distribution network. The principal impacts can be illustrated as in Figure 5.5. Each of the three strategic areas of change required to satisfy a market segment's customer requirements—production, network design, and customer satisfaction targets—contributes to total inventory requirements. Some of the most important factors that tend to increase or decrease inventory requirements are listed next to each of these three areas of strategic change.

Once these impacts are evaluated, an estimate can be made of the total inventory needed to achieve any particular level of customer satisfaction in a market segment. A trade-off is apparent between customer satisfaction and inventory requirements. The company's business strategy and competitive objectives must be considered in assessing the trade-off. The company's financial situation, in particular, its ability to finance the required inventory, should be considered when determining the optimal trade-off between customer satisfaction and inventory requirements.

FIGURE 5–5
What Affects Strategic Inventory Requirements

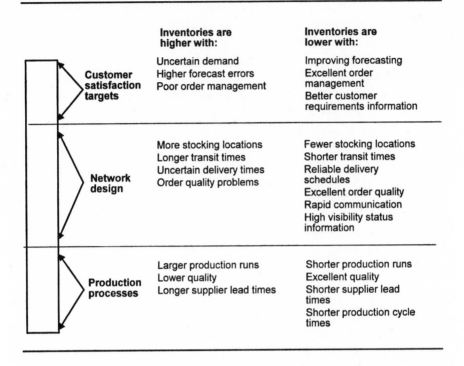

		Inventories are higher with:	Inventories are lower with:
	Customer satisfaction targets	Uncertain demand Higher forecast errors Poor order management	Improving forecasting Excellent order management Better customer requirements information
	Network design	More stocking locations Longer transit times Uncertain delivery times Order quality problems	Fewer stocking locations Shorter transit times Reliable delivery schedules Excellent order quality Rapid communication High visibility status information
	Production processes	Larger production runs Lower quality Longer supplier lead times	Shorter production runs Excellent quality Shorter supplier lead times Shorter production cycle times

At the conclusion of the strategic inventory planning process, the final management decision to be made is whether the prevailing level of customer satisfaction is the right level for the business in each market segment. Strategic business factors will usually aid in this decision. If the performance of the integrated network and the inventory investment made are not achieving the company's customer satisfaction goals, changes must be made. Otherwise, the long-term prospects are loss of market share and possibly declining profits. If performance is acceptable and the return on the working capital invested is equally acceptable, the best option for the business is to continue the overall process of optimizing customer satisfaction at the lowest possible integrated network operating and capital cost.

TACTICAL INVENTORY PLANNING

Earlier we introduced the concept of integrated inventory planning across the network. In Figure 5.2 we saw how the strategic and tactical inventory planning processes worked together to optimize customer satisfaction. In the section above on strategic inventory planning, we discussed the process of optimizing customer satisfaction through changes in production processes, working capital commitments, and network design. Now we will complete the description of the inventory planning process by looking into tactical inventory planing.

While strategic inventory planning can make changes in any or all components of the integrated network, tactical inventory planning seeks to optimize customer satisfaction within the constraints of the company's existing integrated network. When carrying out the tactical inventory planning process, companies work with the existing integrated network, production processes, and sometimes fixed constraints on working capital and operating expenses.

When we isolate the tactical planning process originally shown in Figure 5.2 (the inside circle) we can see that it focuses on satisfying individual customer requirements through the operation of all the network locations—manufacturing, distribution, and customer delivery. The tactical planning process works with existing network locations and the current policies and practices that determine their performance. Included among these policies and practices are production or throughput capacities for each network location, delivery lead times for shipments between locations, and replenishment rules for managing the flow of materials among locations.

Figure 5.6 illustrates the tactical inventory planning process in an integrated manufacturing and distribution company. Tactical inventory planning centers on customer demand. Recall that one of the fundamental goals of the integrated network is to be customer demand-driven for all inventory flows (see Chapter 3). The steps in the process focus on the kinds of actions and measurements companies use to optimize customer satisfaction continuously within the constraints of the existing integrated network.

For the tactical inventory planning process, those steps include setting inventory levels at each network location and establishing the rules that maintain or change them and the rules that manage the flow between locations. Following Figure 5.6, the steps in the tactical inventory planning process are:

FIGURE 5-6
The Tactical Inventory Planning Process

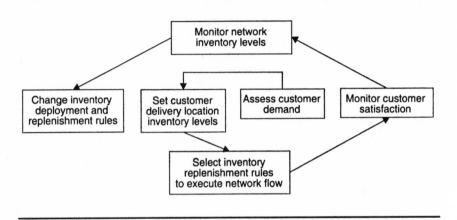

- *Assess customer demand*— For each customer and group of customers served by a network location, measure and analyze the product demand for each product carried in inventory at the location.

- *Set customer delivery location inventory levels*—For each product, determine the level of inventory that will provide desired customer satisfaction on a day-to-day basis for all the customers who purchase the product.

- *Select inventory replenishment rules to execute network flow*—For individual products and groups of products with common sources of replenishment, choose the replenishment rules that will guide decisions regarding when and how much to replenish.

- *Monitor customer satisfaction*—Continuously monitor customer satisfaction with inventory performance measures such as orders filled on-time and complete, backorder and stockout occurrences, and orders diverted to other stocking locations.

- *Monitor network inventory levels*—Continuously measure the total inventory in the integrated network and compare it with targeted levels and measures of customer satisfaction.

- *Change inventory deployment and replenishment rules*—In light of continuously monitored customer satisfaction, inventory in the network, and customer demand patterns, adjust inventory levels and replenishment rules and the locations from which customers are served to optimize customer satisfaction.

Reviewing these six steps in the tactical inventory planning process, we see that this process differs from strategic inventory planning in the following ways:

- Tactical inventory planning focuses on individual customers and all the products they are seeking; the strategic inventory process focuses on individual products and their market segments.
- Tactical planning deals with daily inventory performance and customer satisfaction achievement; strategic inventory planning deals with multiyear planning and the company's competitive position in its market segments.
- Tactical planning works with the existing network, while strategic inventory planning seeks to change the network to achieve optimal customer satisfaction.
- Tactical inventory planning is concerned with the policies and rules that make the best use of the working capital available to finance inventories; strategic inventory planning is concerned with total working capital needed to satisfy each market segment.
- Tactical inventory planning may change operational business processes executed in each network location (inventory replenishment processes, for example); strategic inventory planning is not concerned with operational business processes.

Each of the six steps in tactical inventory planning is described below. The explanations are for a typical product, whose sales have been going on for some time and are expected to continue throughout the tactical planning horizon. Tactical inventory planning must also address other circumstances, such as newly introduced products and products approaching the end of their selling life. We will not consider these situations here.

Assess Customer Demand

One of the concepts that guides inventory management is that good information about customer requirements and product demand is the best substitute for inventory availability. The more we know about customer demand patterns, the better we can carry out the tactical inventory planning process. Earlier we discussed the value of demand forecast information. In assessing customer demand, we want to go well beyond forecasts based on historical projections. Indeed, we want to know our customers' needs as well as we know our own company's needs. In assessing customers' demand we measure the demand for each product for each period in our planning horizon. The best measure of demand for the tactical planning horizon is usually demand over a replenishment lead time.

Seeking detailed information from each customer usually minimizes demand uncertainty. In many companies, demand analysts go straight to the customer and seek out demand information. Many customers have already prepared sales or production plans that represent an accurate forecast of their needs. Knowing, with minimal uncertainty, what demand will appear at each inventory location during the planning horizon is very useful to the company.

Set Customer Delivery Location Inventory Levels

Inventory levels at each location are set for each product according to the demand predicted for the location and the target customer satisfaction desired at the location. Inventory levels may be set according to many different inventory control policies depending on the specific operations of the company and its integrated network. Almost all policies, however, are conceptually equivalent to setting two different inventory levels: a cycle stock level used to cover average or forecast customer demand over a replenishment lead time period and a safety stock level, in addition to the cycle stock, used to assure that no matter what the actual demand, a targeted percentage (usually 99% or more) will be satisfied in accordance with the company's customer satisfaction policies.

Nearly all inventory control policies boil down to this combination of cycle and safety stocks. This is true of so-called min/max rules, order point-order quantity rules, and just about every other type of rule seen in integrated manufacturing and distribution companies. The concept of DRP, or distribution requirements planning, also sets inventory levels in this way in situations where multiple customer delivery locations are replenished from a common source or manufacturing location.

While these inventory control rules predominate, many progressive companies are taking a hard look at their effectiveness. Companies that are adopting the concepts of order management, described in Chapter 3, are changing the way they set inventory levels. They want to take advantage of their order management process's capabilities to seek out supply from the most effective sources on an order-by-order basis. By sourcing the order in the entire network rather than from predetermined stocking locations, many companies have found ways to eliminate stocking locations and source from manufacturing locations alone. Such capabilities come about by applying the strategic inventory planning process described above.

Select Inventory Replenishment Rules to Execute Network Flow

Another important concept in tactical inventory management is managing the flow of inventory throughout the network rather than managing individual stocks in their locations. We know that customer satisfaction is delivered by managing the total flow of materials in the integrated network. Therefore, we know that it is not effective to isolate each stocking location from the network and establish inventory replenishment rules for it as if the rest of the network did not exist.

Inventory replenishment rules are incorporated into the tactical inventory planning process to determine when to order and how much to order. But these traditional rules leave one variable unattended—where to order from. Rather than setting fixed replenishment sources in tactical planning, it is much more effective to make replenishment decisions with a complete view of the entire network. Then the best source or sources of replenishment at the time may be used. It is better to choose sourcing locations from which replenishment will yield maximum customer satisfaction than to force materials to flow through a fixed network regardless of the current stock positions. For example, when unexpected demand at a particular customer delivery location causes a stockout, rather than always looking to the same distribution location for replenishment, companies are looking at the entire network. A company might choose to replenish that customer delivery location from a different distribution location or directly from a manufacturing location, whichever makes sense for customer satisfaction.

Allowing these choices (or exceptions) creates evidence and justification for changing the network in one way or another during the strategic inventory planning process.

Monitor Customer Satisfaction

The tactical inventory planning process is carried out daily in most companies. Up-to-date records of customer satisfaction, measured in order quality and inventory service, provide regular feedback on the performance of the inventories. By monitoring customer satisfaction, managers can make rapid adjustments in their inventory levels, replenishment rules, and other processes that will help maximize customer satisfaction.

Monitor Network Inventory Levels

During tactical inventory planning we expect total inventories in the network to be predictable and consistent with plans made in the strategic inventory planning process. Totals that depart from plan signal that something is not working or that something has changed. Keeping a close watch on total inventories is a critical feature of the tactical inventory planning process. When companies begin experiencing departures from their inventory plans, they must immediately determine the root causes. Most important in root cause analysis is to determine if the situation can be resolved through the tactical inventory planning process. Certain changes in the company's environment can cause total inventories to depart from plan; customer demand could change without warning, or raw materials lead time might lengthen due to supplier problems. In every case, it is critical that the company react immediately to determine the extent and magnitude of impact on customer satisfaction. If the tactical inventory planning process has enough latitude to resolve the situation, the company ought to be able to minimize deterioration in customer satisfaction. If the problems are beyond the tactical planning process, however, more aggressive steps may be needed to preserve customer satisfaction.

Change Inventory Deployment and Replenishment Rules

Continuous comparison of customer satisfaction measures and total inventory in the network will provide a company with the basis for continuously updating its inventory deployment (where to stock and which customers to serve from each location) and its replenishment rules.

CHAPTER 6

PERFORMANCE MEASURES AND MEASUREMENT PROCESSES

Performance measures and measurement processes are approaches to assessing, analyzing, designing, and implementing ways to determine if an integrated manufacturing and distribution network is achieving its objectives. They provide managers with direction and guidance for improving performance. Figure 6.1 shows the basic elements of performance measures and measurement processes. In this illustration, performance measures and measurement processes are the feedback systems used to inform managers about how well their objectives for integrated network performance have been achieved and what must be changed if performance improvements are to continue.

Performance measures themselves are always made up of two parts. The first is:

> *A performance metric*—A selected attribute or criterion, and its units of measure, used to measure performance—for example, customer satisfaction in percent of customers and cycle time in days are performance metrics. The term *performance metric* has been in use for some time now in the corporate world. It provides a way to talk about what managers want to measure rather than the outcome of the measurement.

Performance metrics are managers' choices for what to measure. Managers want to measure performance because it provides the most effective feedback on their business processes—production processes, distribution processes, and customer delivery processes. Usually managers select those metrics that are the best indicators of whether their manufacturing or distribution operations are achieving the objectives set forth in

FIGURE 6–1
Elements of Performance Measures and Measurement Processes

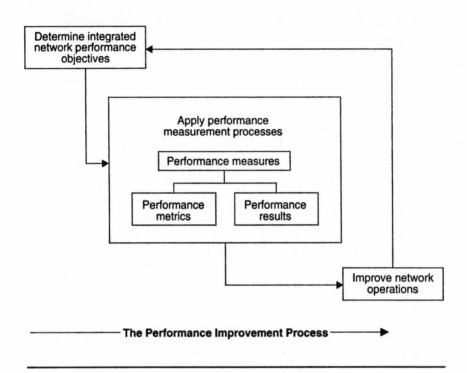

their plans. Many managers find it much more difficult to choose what to measure than to do the actual measuring itself.

The second part of a performance measure is:

A *performance result*—The actual value taken at a given point by a performance metric—for example, last week we achieved 99% customer satisfaction, or our average cycle time yesterday was 2.4 hours.

A performance result changes from time to time. Measurements may be taken only at specified times, such as month end, or they may be continuous, such as customer delivery times. In many cases, a performance result is an estimate of a random variable, such as average cycle time in order fulfillment.

FIGURE 6–2
Fundamental Classes of Performance Metrics

```
1.  Customer satisfaction
2.  Asset utilization
3.  Operating costs
4.  Quality
5.  Cycle time
6   Productivity
```

Performance measurement processes are business processes used to design, implement, and operate performance measuring schemes or systems. Managers apply them to align their performance measures with the business processes they use. For our purposes, we would expect integrated network managers to develop and implement measurement processes that provide feedback on their important business objectives for order management, network management, and inventory management.

Our scope for performance measures and measurement processes will focus on integrated network design and operating objectives. Such objectives are used to measure the success of integrated network strategies. So, for example, if the network strategy were to satisfy customer demand at a lower cost than last year's cost, one of the objectives might be to reduce customer delivery operations cost. In this case, the performance metric would be *customer delivery operations cost*. Performance results (the realizations of the performance metric) are the quantitative means for determining how well integrated network objectives are achieved.

In the integrated network, we will organize all the potential performance metrics managers might use into six fundamental classes or types, illustrated in Figure 6.2. These are:

- *Customer satisfaction*—Performance metrics that are attributes of the company's delivery service that customers value—timely, complete, and accurate delivery.

- *Asset utilization*—Performance metrics whose results are the dollar values or numerical levels of assets in the network, such as facilities, vehicles, equipment, and working capital.

- *Operating costs*—Performance metrics that cover dollar expenses for operating costs of the network, such as labor, maintenance, transport, information services, and rentals.

- *Quality*—Performance metrics whose performance results show conformance or nonconformance to agreed standards in the operation of the integrated network (we will not spend any time on actual product quality here). Examples are errors in deliveries, late shipments, incomplete orders, inventory levels outside of planned ranges, and unreliable activities.

- *Cycle time*—Performance metrics that show the duration of activities or the time between important events, such as the cycle time between the receipt of a customer order and its complete delivery to the customer.

- *Productivity*—Performance metrics that combine two or more measures to create another meaningful performance metric—for example, customer orders *per* facility location, shipments *per* employee, or inventory turns (total shipments divided by average inventory).

In the remainder of this chapter, we will discuss the need for performance metrics in the integrated network, the benefits managers seek from their performance metrics and measurement processes, the range of performance metrics available, and the process for implementing measurement processes or systems.

THE NEED FOR PERFORMANCE METRICS

Performance metrics are needed to determine if objectives are met and to support managers in their decisions about network design, operation, and investments. They are also a basic component of performance improvement. To improve performance in the integrated network, we must measure performance. We know from many life experiences that performance improvements are best achieved by giving managers and workers precise and timely feedback about current performance.

FIGURE 6–3
Two Types of Performance Measurement Processes

Performance Measurement Processes	
Business Results	*Process Results*
· Customer satisfaction	· Quality
· Asset utilization	· Cycle time
· Operating costs	· Activity costs
Productivity	

We need two types of performance measurement processes in the integrated manufacturing and distribution network. Figure 6.3 illustrates that *business results* performance measurement processes offer information about how well the network is performing, and *process results* performance measurement processes provide information about process performance. Business results metrics include customer satisfaction, asset utilization, and operating costs. Process results metrics focus on process performance where quality, activity cost, and cycle time are the three fundamental measures for business process performance.

Productivity is a performance metric that combines business results and process results, so it is shown in Figure 6.3 crossing over both types of measurement processes. Cost metrics are found in both processes. Operating costs, the basic management accounting metric, is a business result usually tied to management organization structure—by department or location, for example. A different kind of cost metric is used for process results. Called activity costs, this metric measures the total cost of an activity or business process no matter where it occurs, crossing over departments or locations. Many companies are finding that activity costs are better than operating cost metrics for performance improvement. Activity costs give a more realistic view of how and why costs are incurred in producing important outputs such as customer satisfaction. A management discipline called *activity-based costing* has grown up around this conclusion in many companies.

Companies need performance metrics and measurement processes for the following common-sense reasons:

- To help understand and reverse deteriorating performance trends that threaten the success of the company.
- To build confidence in the feedback information managers want and use to guide performance improvement.
- To make ongoing measurements of the six fundamental performance metrics listed in Figure 6.2.
- To improve the decision making processes and results that support decisions about integrated network design, change, and investment needs.
- To satisfy managers' continuous need for complete knowledge about network operations so that there are no surprises and their plans can be carried out as originally formulated.

They also need performance measures for higher order reasons—competitive comparisons. Any company operating an integrated manufacturing and distribution network is operating in a competitive environment. To achieve sustained competitive advantages, a company must make performance comparisons between itself and its competition. Those comparisons must use many, if not all, of the same performance metrics the company uses to determine if it is meeting its own objectives or making progress in performance improvements. Otherwise, there is no reliable way to make competitive comparisons.

Making company comparisons using well-defined performance metrics for both business results and process results is often called *benchmarking*. Usually benchmarking involves open and cooperative partners. But the same methods can be applied to competitive comparisons, though the sources of information may be quite different. Benchmarking is also used to help companies identify the right performance metrics to use for either business results or process results. In either case, benchmarking is very useful for:

- Understanding what measurement results constitute competitive advantage for any performance metric.
- Providing insight on performance metric selection.
- Validating objectives that managers believe will help them create or sustain a competitive advantage.
- Gaining a window on how others have achieved a particular measurement result.

• Designing measurement processes that offer the opportunity to use benchmarking to obtain external feedback on business process performance.

BENEFITS OF PERFORMANCE METRICS AND MEASUREMENT PROCESSES

Two important benefits are derived when companies apply performance metrics and measurement processes to the operation of their integrated networks. These are:

• A sense of accomplishment.
• Immediate feedback.

Integrated manufacturing and distribution network operations are large, complex undertakings. Managers with the responsibility for designing networks and achieving network objectives must implement performance measurement before they can find out if they have done the right thing.

Each of the three network processes we covered in the preceding chapters (order management, network management, and inventory management) requires continuous adjustment and change. Each exists in a dynamic environment where both customer needs and external competitive factors change rapidly. Implementing performance metrics and measurement processes is the best way we know to understand and react to the changes. Indeed, we are looking for fast and accurate ways to measure change and react to it. When managers select and implement effective performance metrics, they begin to see how their investment decisions affect the network's performance. Accordingly, they become better at setting objectives.

INTEGRATED NETWORK PERFORMANCE METRICS

In discussing the three integrated network processes, we devoted attention to performance assessment. In Chapter 3, we saw two important steps in the order management process in which performance measurement played a vital part: *prepare order management plans* and *monitor order delivery* (see Figure 3.2). In Chapter 4, we covered network customer service level measures (see Figure 4.5) and network operating costs and investments (see Figure 4.6). In Chapter 5, we devoted time to understanding the network performance information vital to inventory management—cycle time factors, quality factors, and cost factors (see Figure 5.3). We also saw that both strategic and tactical inventory planning depend heavily on performance measurement processes (see Figures 5.4 and 5.6).

In one way or another, we saw that all of our six fundamental classes of performance metrics (see Figure 6.2) are used in every integrated network business process. Let's look at each class and list the range of performance metrics available. In practice, we would expect companies to set target or planned measurement results for most, if not all, performance metrics. We would expect each type of company to select a set of performance metrics consistent with the company's operations, its goals, and the opportunities for performance improvement it sees.

Customer Satisfaction Performance Metrics

The customer satisfaction performance metrics for integrated manufacturing and distribution network processes are:

- Committed delivery date compliance.
- Order completeness.
- Order accuracy.
- Information and communication reliability, accuracy. and timeliness.
- Backorders, stockouts, and fill rates.
- Customer complaints.
- Customer ratings (by survey or inquiry).

Asset Utilization Performance Metrics

Performance metrics for asset utilization in the integrated network are:

- Inventory turnover.
- Working capital employed.
- Average inventory levels.
- Return on assets employed.
- Inventory accuracy.

- Transportation assets employed.
- Facilities assets employed.
- Equipment assets employed.

Operating Cost Performance Metrics

The operating cost performance metrics for integrated manufacturing and distribution network processes are:

- Product acquisition costs (excluding the cost of goods).
- Inbound and outbound transportation costs.
- Quality costs (errors, loss and damage, rework).
- Facility operating costs (product handling and storage).
- Order processing costs (to manage flow in the network between all types of locations).

Quality Performance Metrics

The performance metrics used to measure quality in the integrated network are:

- Forecasting accuracy.
- Schedule compliance.
- Order errors.
- Loss and damage occurrences.
- Customer returns (other than marketing strategy related).

Cycle Time Performance Metrics

The cycle time performance metrics are:

- Order cycle times.
- Inventory review cycle times.
- Customer order processing cycle times.
- Delivery lead times.
- Customer order assembly and documentation cycle times.
- Performance reporting cycle times.
- Production process cycle times.

Productivity Performance Metrics

The range of productivity performance metrics includes:

- Orders processed per time unit (minute, hour, day, week).
- Shipments per facility unit (location, size, personnel unit).
- Input-to-output ratios for product movement or document movement.
- Operating cost measurements per asset unit (cost per location, cost per investment dollar).
- Operating cost measurements per process unit (cost per order, cost per customer).
- Network cost per sales unit (dollars, units).

LESSONS FOR MANAGERS—IMPLEMENTING MEASUREMENT PROCESSES OR SYSTEMS

Implementing measurement processes or systems, like the process of improving the performance of the integrated network, is a process of transition. It is a transitional process because at any point, most companies are using some performance metrics for both business results and process results. The management issue is to make sure that the performance measurement process produces feedback that is relevant to the current objectives and that the measurement process itself performs in an accurate and timely way.

Managers seeking to implement effective measurement processes can look to a four-step process, such as the one illustrated in Figure 6.4, which achieves the transition from current, perhaps less effective performance measurement processes, to improved processes.

Step 1—Assessment

As a first step, managers should assess the current performance measurement processes and systems and determine if the current systems use performance metrics that are relevant for their objectives and if the measurement process provides effective and timely results. Also in this step, managers should take a fresh view of measurement needs for the entire

FIGURE 6–4
Implementing Performance Measurement Processes

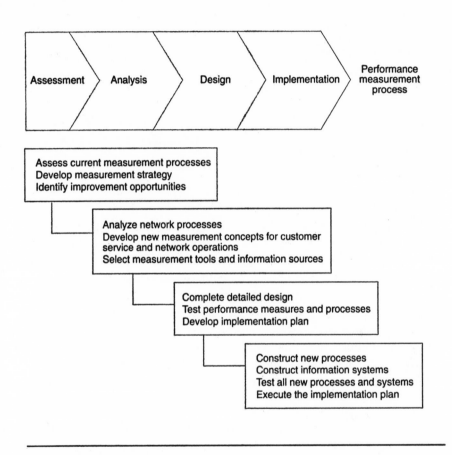

integrated network and all the business processes in the network. Managers should formulate a total integrated network measurement strategy.

This would also be a good time to review the performance of the network processes, because we want to develop better measurement processes but only for effective business processes. The best measurement processes used for poor business processes would do no good.

Step 2—Analysis

Based on the review of the network business processes, managers should develop performance measurement frameworks for every process. Each framework should cover both business results performance measurement and network process results performance measurement. Measurement opportunities should be focused on process-based performance and performance measures that focus on products, market segments, and individual customers.

The measurement strategy developed in the assessment step should be reviewed against the measurement frameworks developed in this step. Do the frameworks fit the strategy? Will new measurement approaches do a better job than the old ones?

Step 3—Design

Performance measurement processes and systems should be designed by the managers who will be using them. The design should address the inputs needed, the information processing required to transform the inputs into desired measurement outputs, and the outputs—especially their accuracy and timeliness. The measurement frameworks developed earlier should now be transformed into instructions or specifications that can be used by information support resources to develop options for implementing the measurement information processing.

Network managers should carefully plan how the new performance measures will be used to support network design and operations decisions.

Step 4—Implementation

The new performance measurement processes should be implemented through information support tools, personnel training, and process validation and approval steps. Thorough testing is a key implementation step.

CHAPTER 7

INFORMATION TECHNOLOGY AND INTEGRATED DISTRIBUTION

Information technology (IT) is the thread running through the enterprise—the link that truly integrates manufacturing distribution and customer delivery. Its innovative use defines the competitive arena, and its role in integrated distributions is that of a key enabler. In other words, it is an integral part of, not a support for, the process. Effective use of IT in the integrated distribution network involves information sharing across operations, using multiple and robust applications linked by a communications network that is flexible and seamless. It is a series of individual applications and technologies linked by common data and networks—a combination of technology and infrastructure. It is not, as many companies unfortunately view it, a "big bang" solution to their business problems, but rather, most effective where it is deployed as an integral part of the company's operations. This does not preclude large enterprisewide applications but requires an ongoing focus on incremental impacts in the company.

This chapter will, therefore, adopt a top down view of information technology in distribution, focusing on several key applications and technologies and their places in an overall IT framework for distribution. Our discussion will address four major topics:

- *IT integration with process*—The information technology enablement of the process. The several process-based philosophies and methods being enthusiastically adopted by supply chain managers must involve information technology to realize their full potential. A framework of integration of IT with process is discussed, along with several examples of different companies' uses of IT in enabling the integrated distribution process.

- *Key applications systems in distribution*—Their primary functionality and use within the context of an overall applications framework for logistics systems.

- *Key success factors in the acquisition and implementation of distribution systems*—Including pitfalls and implementation suggestions, and a justification approach for IT projects.

- *Globalization*—Vis-a-vis integrated distribution systems.

Some information technology and automation issues dealing with specific aspects of distribution operations have been discussed in earlier chapters. This chapter adopts a systemic approach to IT in distribution. Given that distribution is a part of the supply chain, it is rather difficult to restrict the discussion of IT to distribution alone. While we have attempted to do so, it should be realized that, in practice, one must view information technology from an integrated supply chain perspective.

INTEGRATION OF INFORMATION TECHNOLOGY WITH BUSINESS PROCESSES

Information technology is a key enabler (along with organization and performance management) of a company's business processes. As such, its development/acquisition and architecture (its intent and philosophy, essentially) must be totally compatible with the intent and management style it uses to improve or redesign its business processes. This philosophical compatibility is vital if the company is to successfully address the key business issues—managing growth, organization, globalization, cash management, and customer service and response—it faces. And addressing these issues requires the successful integration of information technology with the company's *business focus*—on time/customer/process—and its *management methods*—business process redesign and continuous improvement, total quality management, just-in-time, management through constraints, quick response, etc.

Three aspects of information technology must be addressed:

- Applications systems.
- Decision-support tools.
- Shared information and communications networks for stakeholder/global access.

Very often, companies focus on applications systems without focusing on the necessary management attention on the need for investment in developing a shared information and communications network. One company realized, following years of complaints from the field, that its information systems were inadequate for its current needs; sales were being lost to competitors, customers were turning away because of persistent billing problems and poor quality, and on-time delivery was fast becoming a bad joke among the sales force. Yet, total supply chain inventory was as high as ever. On investigating the problem, managers discovered that while millions had been spent on in-house applications development and modification (often driven by IS-driven user requirements), only a fraction of that amount had been spent in installing a communications infrastructure—an absolute necessity for supply chain communication and visibility. The total bill for remedying that neglect was estimated to be nearly $100 million over a five-year period.

Information technology development will facilitate seamless enterprise systems over the next few years. Deriving a vision of the way in which IT can be integrated into the key elements of the distribution process (process and management methods) for competitive advantage requires that managers step beyond the paradigms of conventional IT thinking in terms of system development methodologies, in-house versus off-the-shelf systems, architecture, and information systems skill sets. Key business processes can no longer be viewed as no more than a combination of process flows and equipment. Information technology developments and the institutionalization of empowerment-based management methods dictate a new perspective—the integration of flows, people, facilities, equipment, and the information technologies required to execute key distribution processes. Figure 7.1 illustrates this perspective of key business processes. The following are examples of companies that have integrated information technologies with processes to make distribution a competitive advantage.

Using information technology, a major medical products company has extended its ordering process through its customers (health organizations) to its consumers (physicians), allowing them to manage their own departmental inventories and replenish directly when stocks run low.

Several large semiconductor firms have extended their distributors' replenishment processes (and their own inventory management process) through information systems into the distributors' warehouses and procurement systems. This allows both the manufacturer and the distributor to check inventory and the distributor to place orders directly.

FIGURE 7–1
Processes—Integration of Process Flows, People, and Information Technology

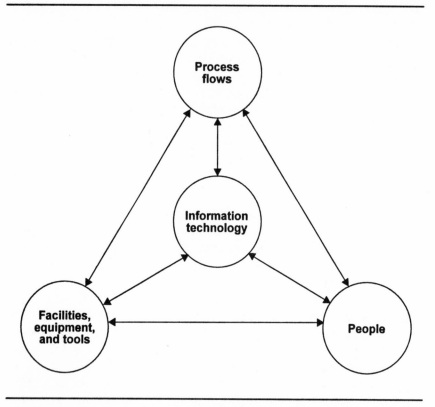

One major electronics company is assessing the state of technology on the market and forecasting technological trends to determine whether key customer-oriented processes (the integration of flows, people, and information technology) must be redesigned to provide a competitive edge in the next decade. In this instance, the process for responding to a request for quote (RFQ) was examined. The RFQ process is depicted across the top half of Figure 7.2. It consists of three distinct sequences: Sequence 1 involved receiving the RFQ from the customer; Sequence 2 consisted of checking product availability, delivery options, configurations, prices, and customer credit lines; and Sequence 3 involved generating a proposal that responded to the RFQ and obtaining (hopefully) the order. The technologies

FIGURE 7-2   An Example: Assessing Technologies for Customer-Oriented Processes

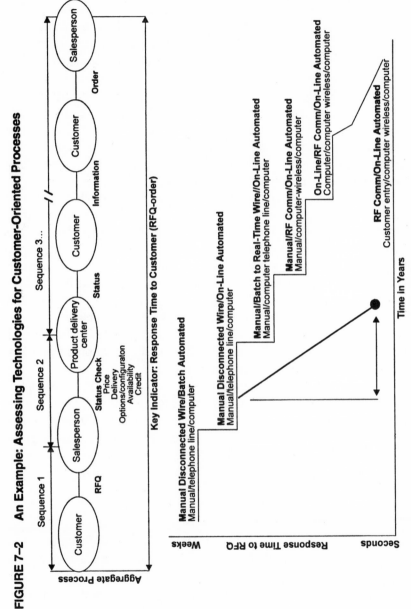

149

that were deemed to have the potential to enable a dramatically improved RFQ response process are depicted in the lower half of Figure 7.2.

The current response time was measured in terms of weeks (the vertical axis) and was enabled by a combination of manual methods and some automation. Sequence 1 was strictly manual; the customer informed the salesperson that the RFQ was being sent, and subsequently, the RFQ was received by mail. Sequence 2 relied on information being transmitted via modem to a central office where capacities, configurations, prices, and credit were checked and computed manually, and the status returned by mail or through the system. Sequence 3 was done via a written document generated locally in a word processing department and mailed (or handed) to the customer's purchasing department. Obtaining the order was a manual effort, resulting in a signed copy of the proposal being returned to the salesperson.

Information technology advancements had made possible electronic transmission of RFQs, sharing standard proposal formats and competitive information, as well as rapid communication between key members of the proposal generating team, regardless of their locations. It was determined that, by providing such technology (laptops, communications hardware and software, and distributed applications to major customers, the market segment sales force, and key members of the account teams) and proposal and solution information on-line to the account team, RFQ delivery and response time could be cut to a few days. This was projected to provide a clear competitive advantage in an industry where speed of response is a key differentiating factor for major corporate accounts.

A large consumer products company replenishes its U.S. retail outlet customers daily, thus reducing pipeline inventory levels while eliminating stockouts. The process makes use of satellite and communications technology for stock visibility and usage management as well as decision-support tools to estimate projected demand based on consumption.

KEY APPLICATIONS SYSTEMS

Distribution applications systems must integrate seamlessly with the other operational systems to enable the integration of distribution activities with those of the entire supply chain. Figure 7.3 describes an overall framework of applications systems within the supply chain and highlights the specific distribution applications within it. There are four levels of applications systems:

FIGURE 7–3
Framework of Supply Chain Applications Systems

There are four levels of application systems:

I	Management reporting									
II	Fore-casting	Aggregate plan/ capacity plan	Prod.plan/ MPS	Procure-ment planning	Inv. status/ WIP control	MRP	Ware-house manage-ment	DRP logic	Routing	Order manage-ment
III	Business planning		Manufacturing resource planning				Distribution requirements planning		Customer service	
IV	Decision support: Modeling Optimization models: Network, inventory deployment									

Level I—Management Reporting

Effective, flexible real-time management reporting (in both summary and detailed formats) is essential for management and monitoring of the supply chain and must be designed into the integrated system—for both periodic and ad hoc information requirements. To be most effective, management reporting must be user-defined and formatted by the decision maker, manager, or analyst, as needed. Systems applications that require extensive lead times for report development and generation are of marginal use in managing the integrated supply chain. Executive information systems (EIS)—the enterprise version of management reporting—must span functions and applications and provide reports for all metrics within the supply chain. New distribution applications must be integrated in terms of database structure and reporting functionality in order to permit the greatest breadth and flexibility of management reporting.

Level II—Operational Applications

Level II applications cover the traditional planning and control functions within the supply chain. These operational applications include forecasting, aggregate planning, production planning and master production scheduling, procurement planning, WIP control and status, material requirements planning, warehouse management systems, distribution requirements planning, routing/route management, and order management. It is at this level that applications integration becomes very important. This section will describe the primary applications in the distribution operation within the context of their use and key functionality. They typically represent modules within larger, more integrated applications systems (Level III applications).

Level III—Integrated Applications

Level III applications are the umbrellas under which the Level II applications fall. They provide the logical, data, and functional integration for the operational applications. They include business planning, manufacturing resource planning, distribution planning, and customer service systems. Our discussion will focus on the distribution planning systems.

Level IV—Decision-Support Systems

Level IV applications are typically add-on systems provided by specialist vendors and require some degree of functional expertise on the part of the company acquiring and implementing them. The primary applications include optimization packages for network configuration and rationalization and modeling packages for inventory deployment. Level IV applications will be addressed briefly in this section.

THE KEYS TO A SUCCESSFUL APPLICATIONS STRATEGY

There are two keys to successfully implementing an applications strategy in the supply chain. Figure 7.4 provides a useful method of categorizing the various supply chain applications based on *decision-making time horizons* and the *scope of the application* involved. Warehouse management systems, for example, involve a relatively short decision-making horizon (within a warehouse shift to a few days for receiving, picking, staging, packing, and shipping) and a fairly narrow scope (local distribution center). On the other hand, distribution requirements planning (DRP II) systems can involve

FIGURE 7–4
Keys to Applications Strategy Success

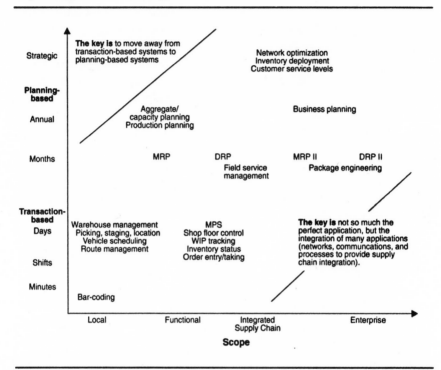

horizons of several months in their decision making and typically span the supply chain. Network optimization models are typically used for strategic decisions that cover the supply chain and can extend to other major processes in the organization (time to market, for example).

The first step in implementing a successful applications strategy is to move away from a transaction-based systems philosophy to a planning-based one. By this, we mean that acquisition of an application must focus on its contribution to planning the operations, rather than on the transactions executed by the system. The acquisition of transaction-based systems can be localized, but the implementation of planning-based applications must be led and managed by a combination of high level business and information systems (IS) managers. The applications involved affect the competitiveness of the company, and their acquisition cannot be delegated to purely functional personnel, whether they be from distribution or IS. Failure to manage this at a high, cross-functional level can, and often does, result in expensive applications, with high switching costs, that do not meet the needs of the business. Indeed, they can harm the company, as processes often have to be modified to fit the system's operations and functionality.

The second key to success is integration. The match of applications functionality to business requirements is not as important as the integration of all the applications through networks, communications standards, and processes. Individual applications, perfectly matched with their respective business requirements, can result in islands of functionality that do not tie together in structure or business process. This is a far, far worse situation than the "75% solutions" that are effectively integrated. Distribution applications systems must be acquired (or developed) with a view toward integration with supply chain and other business applications to provide information access and interchange as part of an enterprisewide IT applications suite.

DISTRIBUTION APPLICATIONS SYSTEMS

Several of the more important operational distribution applications are discussed below. They include distribution requirements planning, financial systems, route management, warehouse management, transportation management, decision support-modeling systems, and field service systems. Some of these applications (for example, DRP and decision support systems) have been discussed in greater depth than the others. This is because companies typically spend a great deal of money and effort in acquiring (procuring and/or developing) these systems, and errors can be very costly in terms of business impact and time wasted.

DISTRIBUTION REQUIREMENTS PLANNING AND THE RELATIONSHIPS OF MRP II AND DRP SYSTEMS

A major component of an integrated logistics system is distribution requirements planning. This is a requirements generation information system that applies material requirements planning (MRP) and time-phased logic to the distribution function.

Consistent with MRP logic, DRP anticipates and aggregates distribution needs through local forecasts and orders from the individual distribution center. Moving backward in the supply chain, the logic then aggregates these demands and, using predetermined rules, allocates specific distribution needs to a specified plant or group of plants (sources). The plants, in turn, use these needs as time-phased requirements or input to the master production schedule.

Figure 7.5 outlines the DRP planning process and the key underlying logic elements. DRP utilizes safety stock and order quantity algorithms as well as source-destination links, allocation rules, and standard lead times to generate its planned requirements. Figure 7.6 outlines the DRP-MRP continuum (linked by the master schedule), while Figure 7.7 illustrates the relationship of DRP and the MRP II system to the planning flow. It can be seen that DRP really closes the loop in the planning of the supply chain. It allows the integration of the distribution, manufacturing, and procurement functions in a single planning chain, and its effective use to plan material flow can ensure that a consistent stream of demand requirements flows through the supply chain. Figure 7.8 outlines some key functional features of a DRP system, categorized into planning parameters, structure and set-up needs, and some key decision-making requirements. The most important areas to examine when acquiring a DRP system are forecasting, network features, distribution requirements planning logic and functions, inventory management, and transportation planning/vehicle loading. These features form the basic elements of a good DRP system.

MRP II systems have very often been sold as "silver bullets" to cure inadequacies in the manufacturing process. It is important that DRP not be viewed in a similar manner, because the distribution process can present the same challenge. Like MRP II, DRP can assist the planning process but can do little to address the basic distribution processes, their capability, or the network structure. Companies must ensure that the distribution and manufacturing processes are capable of producing and delivering product to customer satisfaction. DRP is a planning tool that encompasses a philosophy of doing business that recognizes that all forms of inventory are interrelated. As a management tool, DRP coordinates systemwide planning and flow of material to meet customer service requirements. But, the most important aspect of DRP is its potential to improve the planning of all distribution resources. Successful implementation and use of DRP requires close attention to three aspects of the

FIGURE 7–5
The DRP Planning Process

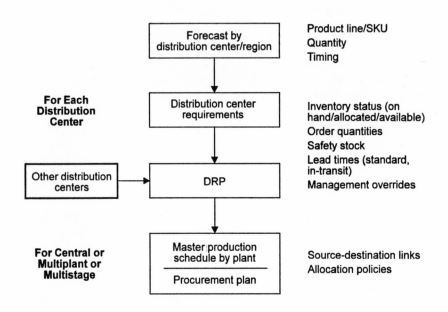

DRP Planning Logic:

For each distribution center, calculate when the on-hand and in-transit inventory will be consumed based on market/forecast requirements (net of allocated).

Use order quantities and safety stocks to calculate planned shipments to each distribution center.

Uses lead times to calculate shipping dates for planned shipments.

Recommend shipments for each source and destination by latest ship dates.

Includes planned shipments and projected on-hand and continues this process to the end of the planning horizon.

Use source-destination links and allocation policies by product for application of logic.

Can suggest alternative shipment routes based on specified rules and parameters.

Source: Christopher Gopal and Gerry Cahill. *Logistics in Manufacturing.* Homewood, IL: Richard D. Irwin, Inc., 1992.

FIGURE 7–6
The DRP-MRP Continuum Linked by the Master Schedule

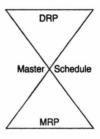

system—the parameters, planning policies, and operating aspects that must be set for effective planning.

These parameters must be set and then analyzed and updated regularly and should include parameters, values, and rules for determining safety stocks by product and distribution center (DC); DC and warehouse capacity standards by product; stocking locations by product; source-destination links by product; and order and ship quantities by product.

Planning policies must be created and implemented to ensure localized responsibility to forecast by DC or region and centralized planning and aggregation with a planning horizon at least greater than the cumulative lead time. These policies must encompass the periodic review and updating of DRP parameters, the setting of enterprise and regional customer service policies, and the assessment and tracking of the forecasting methods used.

A key element of distribution planning is *forecasting*. DRP allows management to transfer forecast responsibility to the regions and/or regional distribution centers—which are, typically, the most knowledgeable about local demands. leading-edge companies use the forecast to drive demand management planning and replanning and use a range of methods to select the one with the best fit in terms of applicability to the business, accuracy, and time horizon. leading-edge forecasting applications provide a range of methods (moving averages, exponential smoothings, Box-Jenkins, trend analysis, and regression, for example) and utilize an open structure to accommodate informed management input and conduct what-if analyses. They are integrated with other systems and often can be linked with, or

FIGURE 7-7
Relationship of MRP, MRP II, and DRP Systems to the Planning Flow

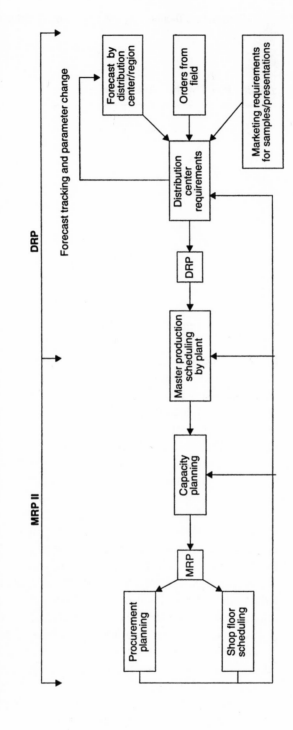

Source: Christopher Gopal and Gerry Cahill. *Logistics in Manufacturing.* Homewood, IL: Richard D. Irwin, Inc., 1992.

FIGURE 7–8

Some Key Features of a DRP System

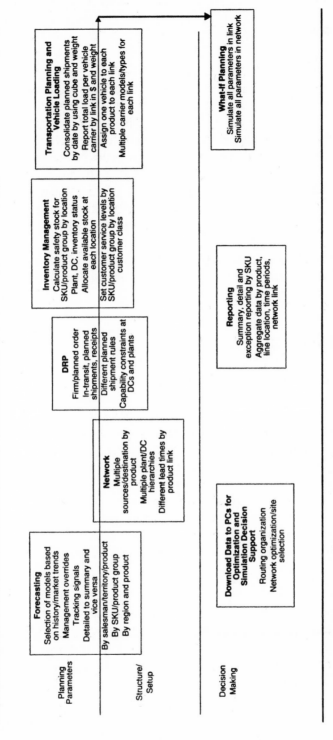

Source: Christopher Gopal and Gerry Cahill. *Logistics in Manufacturing.* Homewood, IL: Richard D. Irwin, Inc., 1992.

actually incorporate, a financial model. For successful planning with DRP, the distribution organization must interface and jointly set policies and forecasts with the other organizational stakeholders. Finally, a process that frequently updates product allocation and effective network flows by product must be developed. The *operational aspects* of the system should include visibility of DC and warehouse stock status by product, source-destination ship schedules, in-transit inventory, shipments and receipts, and expected delivery and receipt dates. Generally speaking, the most important operational issues have to do with accuracy—accuracy of data, system parameters, and the updating process.

The benefits of effectively implementing DRP can be substantial in terms of minimizing inventory investment, improving productivity, and meeting customer service level objectives.

ORDER MANAGEMENT SYSTEMS

Order management systems provide the front-end to the integrated supply chain. As such, they enable the primary customer interface and drive the entire supply chain (see Chapter 3). Because of this, order management applications are receiving the bulk of process reengineering and systems design attention today. While the basic role of an order management application is to permit the easy entry of an accurate order into the system and process it for action along the supply chain, leading-edge companies are focusing their efforts on making it an application that increases competitiveness and customer satisfaction through rapid and accurate order taking, commitment, and turnaround; quick response to customer product requirements; and immediate initiation of supply chain action for delivery. Among the features that leading order management applications possess are:

> • *Ease of order entry*—Orders can be entered via one of several modes—direct on-line terminal by the salesperson and the customer, telephone, electronic interchange, or direct fax input. At the point of order entry, the system prompts the user through the options necessary for accurate order taking and commitment. These include automated, on-line credit checking, which typically involves both external credit checking sources and internal line of credit evaluation. Material availability through the supply chain is

then ascertained. This often starts from the point of inventory closest to the customer (local stocking in a satellite distribution center, for example) and tracks back through the supply chain to the manufacturing schedule. More sophisticated systems check availability through worldwide inventory. This allows accurate commitment of delivery dates and availability. Some leading-edge applications permit pre-allocation of inventory for a specified period, permitting firm commitments until the customer actually confirms the order. At that point, the pre-allocation is turned into a firm order. Finally, the system performs automatic computation of prices, taking into account promotions, discounts, and any applicable special charges. Some systems take into account additional charges for expediting and special shipments.

• *Integration with systems*—Leading order management systems are integrated with other systems, including expert system configurers, production scheduling systems, automated storage/retrieval and warehouse management systems, and inventory replenishment systems. Expert system configurers permit the user to accept customer requirements and, based on these and their priorities, provide a valid configuration of products and accessories, including third-party offerings. The first stage of this process is the matching of requirements against an existing library. If there is no match, the system configures a solution based on the customer's requirements. In the case of build-to-order or out-of-stock situations, the system loads the requirements directly into the master schedule to initiate production and schedule shipment or into the warehouse management system to generate a pick list and shipping instructions.

One large appliance manufacturing company has a system that automatically generates a bill of material, manufacturing drawing, specifications, and routing instructions. In another company, replenishment is automatically computed based on inventory depletion at the particular shipping location.

Order management systems are fast becoming the new arena for providing a competitive advantage. They are, probably, the most important aspect of integrated distribution systems in that they provide the first-line customer interface and can be a major factor in providing a high level of customer satisfaction.

FINANCIAL SYSTEMS

A core application of an integrated supply chain system is the financial and costing system that collects cost data and provides management with effective decision-making information. Care must be taken to ensure, during the planning process, that an integrated mechanism for capturing cost is built into the system. The key to effective supply chain strategy and management is accurate and timely cost and profitability information. Changes—material cost and content, transportation mode and link, volume, and inventory, for example—made to the supply chain must be immediately reflected in the cost data being collected. An activity-based costing system that provides *true* profitability and cost by product is essential in the dynamic environment in which many companies operate today. It must provide information and costs for key cost drivers identified—direct costs as well as indirect and support costs associated with delivery from the supplier to the customer—in other words, true total delivered cost. This includes total costs of customer service by customer class, product profitability, sales return, and volume costs/savings. Above all, the system must be flexible, providing a strategic and operational management tool in addition to performing the traditional role of accounting reporting. The financial system must provide the following information about costing:

- Logistics costs in the areas of product contribution, regional sales/management/support, and customer delivery.
- Accurate and timely reporting of the costs associated with current service levels and increased customer service levels.
- The incremental costs associated with trade-off decisions such as those required to establish optimum service levels and transportation consolidation.
- Periodically recalculated inventory carrying cost to reflect changes in the overhead pool.
- Transportation costs by mode, class, and lane (often through reporting third-party freight cost, and billing services)—if possible, cross-referenced by product, region. and customer.

- All indirect and operating costs associated with the distribution centers, production costs by product and product groups on a plant-by-plant basis, and all administration and order processing costs.
- Ability to incorporate, or download to, a spreadsheet-type analytical package to assess cost trade-offs for strategy formulation and line management.

ROUTE MANAGEMENT SYSTEMS

As empowerment moves to the customer contact points in the organization, route management systems and their integration into the front-end sales and order management process become increasingly important. Such technologies allow business decisions to be made at the driver/salesperson level and must provide a comprehensive level of functionality, including the ability to interface seamlessly in real time with company inventory, management reporting, and marketing systems and manage a variety of channel outlets. A comprehensive application must address driver productivity, customer service, automatic routing and re-routing for efficient deliveries and pick-ups, invoice and manifest generation, flexible dispatch capabilities, and on-line communication with the driver/salesperson. The key functionality categories that route management applications must provide are:

- R/F communication with remote systems coupled with palmtop and laptop computers for ease of data entry and information reporting. This can involve communication capabilities on trucks designed to maintain up-to-the-minute information and communicate with dispatch headquarters or distribution centers. Frito-Lay uses such technology in managing their routes.
- Functionality that enables the driver/salesperson to add value to his customers' processes. This includes technologies such as bar coding, which helps manage customers' inventory. As route salespeople move toward increased value-added services (assisting their customers in inventory replenishment and managing inventory and shelf space, for example), such functionality is important in obtaining stocking information and providing shelf space and replenishment guidelines. This

can be a powerful tool for increasing customer dependence and switching costs. The functionality should also use decision support tools that can assist customer and salesperson profitability by mix and shelf space. Finally, such systems must allow the driver to collect competitive information on shelf space, product, and stocking.

- Financial capabilities to include route accounting, provide information for financial accounting and profit analysis (by route and product), feeds to accounts receivable and driver settlements applications. The financial functionality must include comprehensive reporting by distribution/pick-up route and store.

- Inventory replenishment assistance to include sales forecasting, analysis and reporting, inventory control and order tracking, placement reporting, and promotion and discount management.

- Automated (computer-assisted) dispatch that can assign pick-ups and deliveries automatically in the most efficient manner (based on route, driver availability and proximity, size of shipment, etc.) and communicate the assignments to the driver in the truck. This involves real-time tracking of truck location and manifest generation at the time of routing. The routing itself must be flexible and allow, on a daily basis, for volume changes, vacations, and truck availability.

- Automatic invoice generation at the customer location.

- An intuitive user interface that can be used by people who are not highly systems-literate. This includes checklist-driven menus, a graphical interface, and as much embedded intelligence as possible.

Many companies now provide their sales forces with these technologies in varying degrees of sophistication and complexity. In some instances, the technology enables drivers/salespeople to behave like company-owned franchises, making their own business, inventory, and credit decisions within broad guidelines and receiving compensation based on profitability and performance. Such salespeople typically have on-line access to company-level sales and profit reporting and tracking. Using such systems, the driver/salesperson can be the competitive frontline for the company, triggering replenishment orders by SKU back along the supply chain, based on actual customer needs and sales. Many provide high value-added services by assuming the traditional customer/store functions of inventory management, shelf layout, and product profitability analysis, thereby creating high switching costs and high barriers to entry for competitors.

WAREHOUSE MANAGEMENT SYSTEMS

The warehouse management system enables a core piece of the overall order management process. It is essential for rapid and accurate order turnaround and finished goods management. The transactions that take place at a distribution center include receipt of products and other materials, movement of material to various locations (inspection, stores, price ticketing, replenishment, etc.), repackaging, location order and storage consolidation, picking, staging, and arranging for shipment (loading for stop sequencing, routing, etc.). At a large distribution center, an enormous number of these transactions must be initiated, monitored, and completed, all in very competitive times and at low costs. Management methods such as just-in-time, while reducing the amount of material stored, have greatly increased the number of transactions, through increased (though smaller) receipts and more frequent shipments. Material is now released on demand, rather than on a fixed schedule. This has vastly increased the complexity required of a warehouse management system. Leading applications are now almost fully automated, from receipt through shipment, to cope with this complexity and provide rapid order turnaround and high productivity.

A warehouse management system is best described in terms of its core functionality. It is important to note that this functionality must be integrated; it should not become a series of "islands of automation" located throughout the distribution center. At an aggregate level, the warehouse management system must:

- *Enhance order turnaround by accepting* orders and notices of scheduled receipts electronically (including via satellite communication) and manually from the field and feed them directly into the distribution center operations for action. To do this, it must provide visibility of all items in stock and scheduled receipts; identify the flow of material through the system, matching product and lot information with customer, order, and purchase order information (i.e., maintain lot genealogy and tracking); and be able to suggest and implement substitution when requested items are unavailable. To this end, it must support bar coding; handle a variety of pricing plans, deals, promotions, and rebates; and provide packaging rules and guidelines (master cartons, palletization, etc.) for different products. More sophisticated systems use order and receipt information to drive storage/retrieval automation for storage, retrieval, consolidation, and picking operations.

- *Enhance distribution center operations by* providing locator rules and capability in the warehouse, enabling picking and staging, and generating accurate and timely shipping documentation and invoices. More sophisticated systems can provide guidance on "best door" selection for receiving material. In addition, the system must provide the capability to reserve inventory in stock and sign inventory in and out when the goods are consigned. The application must also be capable of managing and controlling warehouse product and packaging inventory through perpetual inventory and physical inventory checks/audits, while valuing and tracking inventory costs to assign true cost of inventory at the time of sale. Such systems must be able to handle federal, state, and local taxes as well as international shipping and customs regulations (including bonded items). The complexity of these transactions grows exponentially as the scope of distribution center operations expands from regional to national to global. Finally, such applications must support such methods as cross docking.

- *Handle second order operations*, such as partial and over-shipments, returned material and damaged goods, accounting for them, and returning them to source.

- *Communicate with, and drive, warehouse automation, including* automated storage/retrieval systems. Some of these technologies include automatic high speed sorters, vision systems, light-aided order picking, and voice-aided input and output. In addition, the system must be able to communicate with customer and supplier systems. It is the frontline to the customer and must, therefore, provide all the necessary management and status reporting information, making it accessible to all parts of the enterprise. In certain industries, a warehouse management system can provide a major competitive advantage through rapid order turnaround and replenishment and increases in warehouse productivity. One retail clothing company, for example, has installed a highly sophisticated and automated system that includes automatic receiving, storage, picking, staging, and replenishment. The system includes continuously rotating storage racks under computer control and manages virtually all material movement, with workers involved only in packaging and disposing of packaging material and loading for shipment. As a result, the company has been able to ship its orders 100% on time, with very high degrees of accuracy and completeness. In the process, it has achieved extremely high levels of productivity and distribution center throughput.

It can be seen that the warehousing management system deals with all the complexity inherent in the business and must be integrated with all components of the distribution system and the primary operational and financial (accounts payable, accounts receivable, general ledger) systems. In many industries, it forms the core of a company's business system.

TRANSPORTATION MANAGEMENT SYSTEMS

The transportation operation is the end point of the delivery chain. As such, effective management and accuracy are key to the operation. A transportation management system must, therefore, support all the customer-driven delivery requirements as well as company goals for delivery costs and service. Among the primary functions that the system should support are:

- Planning and monitoring of in-transit, interplant, customer, and supplier shipments and material expediting from different locations.

- Contract administration, carrier selection, monitoring of carrier performance, and evaluation.

- Freight billing (and managing third-party freight billing systems) and management of government regulations, including union rules, cross-border regulations, customs, and export documentation.

- Transportation scheduling and routing (including computerized routing and dispatch), including planning and automated replanning for numbers of trucks, containers, etc., and cost efficiencies such as shipment consolidations, continuous runs, and backhauls. Also important is fleet management, including maintenance and replacement, lease and purchase options, and the transport of hazardous materials. While the system must plan for vehicle loading for maximum utilization and delivery efficiencies, it must also accommodate customer-defined transportation modes and delivery preferences.

Several companies are now utilizing advanced communication technologies for carrier and shipment monitoring. These companies are replacing their voice radio dispatch operations with on-board computers using radio data networks, which allow dispatchers to communicate directly and accurately with drivers, even when drivers are not in their vehicles. These systems contain computerized routing/dispatch applications with complete city maps and street address locations and provide an integrated transportation management system. Because these carriers often represent the company to the customer, monitoring their performance is essential for total customer satisfaction.

FIELD SERVICE APPLICATIONS

Recent, highly visible surveys of several computer companies have demonstrated the strategic importance of field service. In order to support a high, competitive level of service, it is essential that the manufacturer acquire and implement a field service system that is integrated on a worldwide basis with logistics, sales/marketing, engineering, and manufacturing. While field service is covered elsewhere in this CIRM series, it deserves some discussion here because of its impact on distribution. Of particular importance in such a system is the ability to manage a variety of service requirements that affect the replenishment and distribution of spares and service components. These requirements include on-line diagnostic analysis, MTBF (mean time between failure) analysis and breakdown frequency, prediction of service calls, and replacement before actual breakdown. This results in proactive field inventory management and planning (including OEMs, spares, and peripherals) and replenishment policies based on replacement analysis from the field. Field service systems must be integrated with engineering and manufacturing systems to manage new product introduction (and product phase-out), availability of spares, and delivery requirements.

Often ignored (relatively speaking) in favor of manufacturing and materials systems, field service applications are today *the* key factor in influencing repeat sales, as study after study shows that after-sales service is an important component of the customer's buying decision. Defining and developing such a system, therefore, requires the active participation of engineering, marketing, manufacturing, and distribution functional personnel.

DECISION SUPPORT—MODELING SYSTEMS

Three types of decision-support tools assist management in making and evaluating distribution decisions. They involve constructing models of the integrated supply chain (see Chapter 4) and evaluating them using what-if analysis, sensitivity and flexibility analysis, in an iterative approach whose major purpose is to develop management commitment. The objective is usually to minimize total network costs at competitive speed and customer service levels. Modeling can be used to optimize distribution operations and, on a wider basis, the entire supply chain. Typical applications include:

- Local routing and distribution optimization.
- Product mix supply-demand to balance global resources.
- Inventory deployment and trade-offs with customer service levels.
- Network configuration and flows.

These models require a definition of the current operations baseline in terms of costs, flows, service levels, and volumes and must include product phase-in/out plans and projected demand schedules. They can be developed based on the constraints and guidelines identified during the logistics strategy planning process (proximity/time and market preferences, for example) and the options identified as strategically desirable. Alternatively, some firms first develop a range of solutions and then evaluate them based on their response to competitive factors. The different modeling approaches that can be used (and their selection depends on the complexity of the firm's distribution environment) include optimization, heuristic modeling, simulation, and financial modeling.

Optimization models are mathematical programming tools that attempt to optimize for minimum cost, maximum profit, or maximized services levels. They are used in inventory deployment, network configuration and rationalization and, through simulation, determining optimal product mix policies given various business and cost constraints. They are excellent what-if tools and are useful in managing high capacity, product and resource constrained situations. These models assist decision making and provide solutions to such problems as:

- The number of distribution centers and stocking locations required, their location and purpose (mission, size and function).
- The product lines, mix, inventory stocking levels, and safety stocks at each location.
- The management and deployment of this inventory for changes in product line and market demand.
- The combination of transportation modes (rail, sea, air, truckload, LTL, overnight, etc.) as well as issues involving customer pick-up and delivery, which can cost-effectively be used to meet demands of time, delivery frequency, and quantity.
- Product flows from sources to destinations.
- Costs to maintain and improve customer service levels along different dimensions and the impact of, and sensitivity to, major distribution cost drivers.
- Evaluation of the risks that, if they occurred, would significantly affect customer service levels, delivery time, speed, and cost.

The success of these models as decision-making tools depends on model construction and set-up to handle potentially misleading parameters, such as semifixed and semivariable costs. Such models can help managers address complex problems as well as uncover options not readily obvious at first glance. The several excellent modeling packages available range from stand-alone personal computer software to specialized logistics optimization packages that can download data from company databases. Their disadvantages lie in their complexity to develop and maintain and their inherent weaknesses in modeling essentially qualitative and strategic parameters such as process staging and market preferences.

Heuristic models are based on, as the name suggests, heuristics, or informed rules of thumb. An example of a commonly used heuristic is that all customers in a particular area will be served by a particular plant.

Heuristic modeling cannot produce the range of solutions, or the optimum solution, that optimization modeling can. It does, however, reflect the experience and judgment of management, which is an important factor in any distribution decision. These rules, however, may reflect traditional mindsets and, therefore, not be the best for competing effectively or satisfying customers in the new era.

Simulation models simulate different scenarios provided by company management and compare them for cost, profit, and time. A disadvantage, as in heuristic modeling, is the use of pre-determined scenarios that may not reflect future outcomes.

Financial, or operational, models are usually utilized when the problem is localized—a small company's distribution operation or the distribution implications of a particular brand or geographical area, for example. They often consist of spreadsheet-type models and accept pre-determined scenarios which are then compared for performance. To be effective, their output must include cash flow and profit and loss statements reflecting the different scenarios and what-if changes.

All these modeling techniques must have, as a prerequisite, rigorous cost and performance baseline models that include direct and indirect costs and their allocation (through major cost drivers). In addition, the baseline must be accurate in its portrayal of product flows, volumes, demand, and inventory levels. Supply chain modeling is not totally scientific; the models must be developed with business needs in mind. Too much aggregation will result in high-level information that may not be useful for decision making, while too much detail (by individual SKUs and customers, for example) creates a model that is very costly to build and maintain and probably provides only a small incremental benefit. Further, the level of data that may be required in a highly disaggregated model will probably not exist in the firm, or it will cost too much to collect and update. Such data can include the modes of transportation used among lanes, state and local government requirements, union rules, types and frequency of delivery required by customers, and a host of other variables. At a higher level of aggregation, such information can be estimated reasonably well with structured questionnaire tools. The key, therefore, is to strike a balance that provides useful decisionmaking information at a reasonable cost and maintenance level.

Figure 7.9 provides the decision support (functional and interface) requirements of a sophisticated supply chain optimization model. These requirements were developed for a global consumer electronics company

FIGURE 7-9

Name	Network Optimization/ Rationalization	General Description of Module	Optimization Model to Provide Least Total Cost Solutions/Options under Various Changeable Contraints through What-If and Sensitivity Analysis

Critical Success Factors

- Accurate cost, volume and projection data
- Model parameters and constraints from senior management
- Attributable product line cost allocation
- Ongoing in-house use/maintenance know-how

Information Required

- Production and distribution costs by product—direct/indirect and support
- Demand volumes and customer/regions by product
- Transportation data (lanes, modes, volumes/weights, rates including overnight and two-day air)
- Delivery preferences and market data
- Source-destination links and OEMs
- Cycle times across supply chain
- New product introduction/phase-out plans and projections

Key Decisions

- Manufacturing plant location and parameters (product mix/volume)
- Distribution center location, type (service, break-bulk, etc.), parameters, products, stocking levels, throughput
- Transportation flows (Plant-DC, interplant, inter-DC, DC-customers/regions by product, source-destination links by product)
- Plant-DC rationalization

Information Produced

Network
- Manufacturing plant/DC product mix and rationalization
- Source-destination links (Plant-DC-Customer/Region)
- Graphical display—maps, lanes, distances

Market
- Demand pattern analysis by order size, frequency, sales volumes, weights, cubes, geography
- Seasonality with flexible time buckets

Financial
- Incremental cost differentials—one-time/ongoing
- Link to plant level/corporate P&Ls
- Total network costs by stages, source-destination links, fixed, semifixed, and variable costs
- Warehousing and inventory costs

What-If and Sensitivity Analysis

Changes
- Demand and customer regions
- Transportation rates
- Operating and material costs
- Source-destination links

Products
- Product mix by plant
- New product introduction/phase-out
- Capacities expansion—plant/DCs

Sensitivity analysis

Demand
- Cost vs. customer levels
- Cost vs. stocking locations
- Cost structures—key inputs

Technology Interfaces

- Costing system
- Demand management/supply demand planning system
- Order management system
- Marketing data systems (internal/external)
- Production databases
- DRP system

Constraints

Capacities
Throughputs
- Customer service levels/fill rates
- Unique supply-demand regional characteristics
- Source-destination links not permitted
- Specialized storage/transport/plant/DC requirements
- Product-process mix for plants
- Unique proximity requirements

Key Operational Issues

- Number and location of Plants/DCs
- Plant and DC parameters
- Product mix and volumes, throughputs
- Inventory deployment
- Source-destination links (Plant-DC-DC-customer/region/product)

Technology Issues

- Data downloading/uploading
- File compatability

Risk Management Issues

- Validate assumptions periodically
- Run and evaluate model periodically for validation and changes
- Track demand patterns for changes
- Develop in-house logistics modeling capabilities

that used a variety of distribution modes and had a widely dispersed network of manufacturing plants, OEMs, distribution centers, and contract warehouses. While not every company will need an application of this magnitude and sophistication, the requirements provide a useful guideline for the various elements that are required of an optimization package. Of particular importance are the requirements for interface and connectivity with company databases and other systems and for ongoing in-house use and maintenance of the system, which involves training and education in construction, update, and evaluation of output. Ideally, in-house personnel and line management will be trained to use the model and to change the parameters and structure to reflect business conditions.

APPLICATIONS INTEGRATION

Essentially, applications integration is achieved through three major technology enablers—shared databases and database technology, communications networks, and electronic data interchange (EDI). These are discussed briefly below.

Shared database and networks provide the supply chain with common, easily accessible information. An increasing number of leading-edge companies are experimenting with the concept of *the information warehouse.* An information warehouse may be a single database or a large number of databases throughout the supply chain, indeed, the enterprise, connected by technologies that make them transparent to the user. Such shared information, which is essential if the supply chain is to be integrated, consists of common customer information with common customer numbers, sales/geography, inventory status, shipment delivery, and transportation status information. It is required across functions, geographical regions, market segments, and customer locations as well as across management levels. As the value of information as an asset grows in importance, the relative value of physical assets decreases; such shared information is gaining importance as a source of competitive advantage. Successful companies have recognized this and acted on it with aggressive information technology and communications strategies that encompass state-of-the-art technologies such as cellular voice and data and include innovative uses of communications technologies such as satellites.

While return on information (ROIn) is a measurement that exists only in concept and has yet to be defined and adopted by companies, return on management (ROM) is gaining increased acceptance, and its measurement is being experimented with by some leading companies. Management in this context involves managing integrated information, processes, and people to meet customer needs and provide a sustained competitive advantage.

While database technologies provide the ability to store, retrieve, and manage information and communication technologies permit the sharing and transmission of that information, *electronic data interchange* is the tool that creates the linkages among the various stakeholders in the dispersed supply chain. EDI can take several forms and protocols and it enables the alliances and partnerships necessary for success. EDI is the integrative technology for the virtual supply chain. While extensively used in situations involving large volumes of business transactions and data tracking requirements, it is increasingly used by firms to link their supply chains and construct the virtual factory (integrating suppliers, customers, third parties, geographically dispersed operations and functions). Figure 7.10 illustrates some of the information that companies are transmitting through the use of EDI along the virtual supply chain. It can be seen that practically all product- and order-related communications are sent, or can be sent, via EDI to achieve the following benefits:

- *Reduce time* in communication with suppliers and customers, and within geographically dispersed manufacturing and distribution locations (for example, schedules, plans, material and engineering change releases, etc.).

- *Increase accuracy* of communication regarding orders, inventory status and visibility, engineering and supplier product and process designs, and customer requirements.

- *Streamline transaction-based operations* (order entry, accounts receivable, and accounts payable).

- *Reduce redundancy* of data flowing from one entity to another along the supply chain.

- *Increase response* in order fulfillment, supply management (delivery, design, location), and schedule changes within the network.

- Indirectly, to *reduce pipeline inventory levels, improve sales productivity,* and, in general, *improve customer service levels.*

FIGURE 7-10
EDI Use along the Virtual Supply Chain—Some Examples

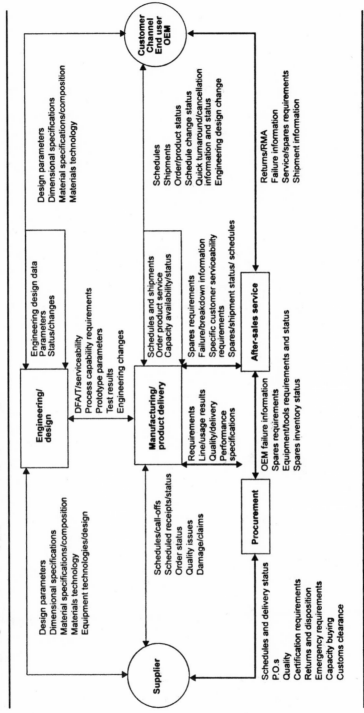

Source: Ernst & Young Center for Information Technology & Strategy: All Rights Reserved.

175

The adoption of EDI is, by no means, a simple technology decision. It involves several major IT and organizational issues, including:

- *Information sharing*—Information is power inside an organization and even more so outside the organization along the supply chain; it can threaten organizational relationships. One major supplier of a large company hedged on its EDI commitment for a long time; it did not want to reveal its true schedules and stock status to the customer. This resistance broke down after the customer threatened to reduce its volume of purchases unless the supplier agreed to its linkage terms. EDI must be a mutually agreed upon strategy, with firm definitions of the data to be transmitted, its periodicity, and its content. Where the data is subject to manipulation, it is sometimes necessary to link databases. The benefits of EDI, therefore, must be articulated and made clear to all the parties. One large computer manufacturer, for example, has written connectivity requirements into its purchase agreements for suppliers and has taken pains to explain the mutual benefits.

- *Standards*—Standards must be set carefully after reviewing the operating environment and the industries involved. EDI standards are often industry-dependent, and clear standards and agreements must be defined regarding standards, data elements, and transaction sets. Similarly, multinational firms will probably have to implement more than one standard. Several companies have developed "EDI black boxes" that can handle a variety of standards.

- *Applications and communications*—It is important to review current applications and communications networks within the company for integration, standardization of data within the company, and the systems' abilities to support EDI standards. EDI facilitates functional and, therefore, information integration. Given this, many companies are centralizing their evaluation and standards-setting on an enterprisewide basis. The company must proceed carefully before investing in conversion or translation applications. They must be flexible and capable of supporting multiple EDI standards, control and report capabilities, interfaces with existing hardware and software, and security.

Some of the specific issues that must be resolved include *communication* (time zones, communications protocols, hardware types), *data standards* (user data standards, cross-industry standards, and maintenance of standards), and the *EDI environment* (implementation with trading partners, applications interfaces, and translation issues involving the host, network, and front-end). The major issues, though, revolve around organizational implementation and are similar to those encountered in any implementation of integrative technology. Companies must, however, guard against acquiring technology for technology's sake. Not all implementations of EDI have proved effective, and the objectives, costs, benefits, and protocols must be evaluated carefully. Company standards must be adhered to, and customers must be actively involved in the process to ascertain and incorporate their needs and standards. This ensures a partnership and provides strategic benefits to both the manufacturer and the customer (providing a mechanism for rapid response and reducing the time to market for new products). Several large components manufacturers have linked their supply databases (inventory status, allocation, availability) to those of their distributors (stock status, demand, orders) in order to ensure end customer satisfaction through service and availability, using low pipeline inventory levels.

KEY SUCCESS FACTORS IN THE ACQUISITION AND IMPLEMENTATION OF DISTRIBUTION SYSTEMS

Successful IT planning and decisions to acquire systems or develop them in-house are important in the rapid and effective introduction of information systems in an integrated distribution and manufacturing company.

Information Technology Planning

Several factors govern the success of information technology planning and design. First, senior management must be completely convinced of the merits of the entire effort. They must also communicate their commitment, in word and action, to all personnel involved, the corporate stakeholders affected by the integration of information, the customers, and the distributors.. Second, system users must be actively involved throughout the planning process. They must participate in the design effort to insure ultimate success (a term used by one major company for this involvement is "submersed"). Project team members should be committed full-time to the effort. Often, whole segments of a planning effort weaken or fail due to lack of team participation. Management must dictate the necessity, and instill the importance, of full-time participation. Core members of the project team must represent, at a minimum, the primary organizational entities within integrated distribution functions. Representative experts from external stakeholders at various points in the process (customers, transportation companies, contract warehouses) should also be included. The project team selected must be cross-functional and empowered to remove departmental barriers. In an effort as important as IT planning, such barriers can be detrimental to the company's competitiveness and success. Classic departmental barriers include information hoarding, multiple databases with duplicate data, nonintegratable and incompatible applications, and the IS policy of undertaking every IT application as an in-house development effort.

Off-the-shelf Software versus Customer-Developed versus In-House-Developed Software

Sooner or later in the planning process, the company will have to deal with the decision of choosing the most effective and rapid means for building the system. Several factors are involved in this decision:

- The size and complexity of the supply chain and its requirements.
- Current information systems in place.
- Availability of software applications packages and hardware migration paths.
- Confidence in vendor and/or in-house capability.
- Resources in terms of capital and timing, people and time.

There are significant advantages to acquiring (and later modifying or enhancing) off-the-shelf applications packages. Vendors have already developed a great deal of the functionality, and it does not make a great deal of sense for the in-house information systems department to duplicate their efforts. In addition, good packages are flexible and can easily be tailored to user requirements, and unlike many in-house developed systems, third-party applications software is well documented and supported with maintenance and future enhancements. Third-party applications can almost always be had for a lower overall cost, which includes the overhead of maintaining an applications development staff, and their immediate acquisition results in more rapid implementation which, in turn, ensures quicker results.

Similarly, there are some significant disadvantages to developing software in-house. In-house IS systems analysts often lack the functional expertise that software vendors invest in, and turnover in IS departments could contribute to time and cost overruns. Because of these factors, in-house developed systems are usually more costly in terms of money and time to build and maintain. In addition, their rigid coding does not allow for flexibility, and in-house documentation during development and future enhancement is often poor.

IS weakness notwithstanding, if the integrated distribution systems and process are core competencies of the organization and provide a proprietary competitive advantage, it makes sense to develop the systems in-house. In such instances, the company must invest in the skills, development tools, and methodologies necessary to provide the bases for development.

Successful Implementation

Successful implementation can be defined as a combination of organizational acceptance and tangible results—reduced inventory, increased customer service levels, tighter alliances with stakeholders, improved decision making, etc.) obtained from the implementation of the system. The components of success include:

- *The right system*—The right system includes the information technology that has the necessary features for the processes involved, ease of use, migration path, flexibility and integration capabilities, technical and functional support. One of the great myths in systems definition is that "the users know what they want." Typically, the users know their requirements for automating and extending their current processes. It is imperative that IT definition be the result of a business vision and incorporate an examination of the processes involved.

- *Education*—The old adage, "If you think education is expensive, try ignorance," still holds true. Lack of education is the primary cause of IT implementation failures. Education is expensive—it involves the cost (and opportunity cost) of people's time, training and trainers, and training materials and facilities. Education must encompass functional education and IT system-use training as well as cross-disciplinary education. This last involves addressing the questions: "What decisions do I make that would have an impact on other functions?" "What is the type and level of this impact?" "What decisions made by others affect me?" And, finally, "What do my internal suppliers and customers require of me?"

- *Communication*—The communication of policies and results of reviews is essential for successful system implementation. However, communication must be coupled with *management commitment* to the requirements of success, including education, resource allocation, and a realistic expectation of results. IT involves change, and communication and commitment must be backed up by *management willingness to foster change* and set in place the necessary infrastructure to accommodate and manage change. Change is risky—a moving away from the status quo—and the commitment to undertake reasoned risks must be an integral part of IT implementation.

- *Involvement of all concerned*—Traditional implementation wisdom defines this aspect as *user involvement*. It is much more than that; it requires the active involvement and participation of higher-level management, IS, users, support/indirect personnel, and other functional groups within integrated distribution management and operations.

- *Implementation organization*—The infrastructure and decision-making roles necessary to successfully implement a major information system must include senior management to set direction and be the arbiter of strategic viability and resource allocation, an overview management structure for the implementation process, and cross-functional representation and involvement to ensure organizational and supply chain management success. Figure 7.11 depicts one such organization structure for the implementation of a logistics information system in a large manufacturing firm. It can be seen that the Implementation Team is empowered to assess alternatives, while the Implementation Committee sets policy and reviews recommendations. The role of the Steering Committee is to arrange for organizational interventions—inclusion in the budget, obtaining resources,

FIGURE 7–11
An Implementation Organization

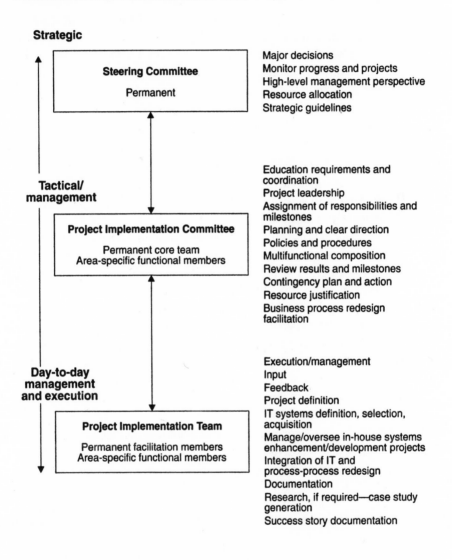

and driving the change management required for a major systems acquisition and implementation. This includes communication and emphasis on senior management commitment. This structure worked very well and resulted in the identification of a system within three months and a contract within four months of the start of the effort.

Finally, successful IT implementation requires a *detailed project plan* (with timelines, milestones, deliverables, roles, and responsibilities) and a budget to measure and monitor time and cost.

Some suggestions for successful implementation include:

- *Start with the easiest*—An integral part of implementation success is organizational acceptance. The organization must be convinced that the effort will be successful, and obtaining early success is an excellent way to achieve this. Another aspect of this strategy is to implement in steps to obtain better project control and the necessary early benefits and payback.

- *Plan and execute for a quick implementation*—The traditional 18- to 24-month timelines associated with implementation prevailed during a period of relatively low IT sophistication. Furthermore, industry and competitive dynamics now change so rapidly that IT should not become the bottleneck or constraining factor. A six to 12 month time period would be an aggressive target.

- *Try initially for an 80% solution*—A comprehensive, 100% solution is likely to take an inordinately long time, probably causing management and the users (and suppliers and customers along the supply chain) to lose interest. The incremental balance of the benefits will accrue in due course.

- *Integrate projects, people, and technology*—If projects are developed in a vacuum, the system will lose its cost and impact efficiencies. Try to involve customers. Customers should be invited to share in the implementation effort. They are more likely to incorporate compatible systems, extend existing systems, or invest in new technologies if they see benefits in the links to their supplier's order fulfillment systems.

- *Plan for flexibility*—Working capital is required to begin the investment process. Building new IT systems can be very expensive, and while procuring them may be less expensive, it is only a matter of degree. However, good planning will reduce the likelihood of unexpected overruns. The effects of external fiscal pressures on implementation can also be reduced by careful monitoring and quick alteration of plans. It is essential, therefore, that the plans be well developed and robust to permit such changes in direction or emphasis.

In the final analysis, successful implementation of a major information system in integrated distribution management depends upon achieving cross-functional integration and planning.

Implementation Pitfalls

There are several pitfalls that can lead to failure of the IT planning and implementation process. Chief among these is the lack of commitment of the executive management team to the process. Lack of a coherent, documented, and articulated competitive strategy nullifies the effort. Other pitfalls that must be avoided include:

- *Incomplete methods and tools*—The software design and selection methods do not address all current and future business needs, or the distribution network definition is incomplete. Very often, the inventory management approaches (lead times, policies, parameters, forecasting tools) are inadequate for the business needs. In addition, many companies fail to fully comprehend the hardware and software integration effort required, and documentation is quite inadequate for training, future use, or modification.

- *IT perceived as a tool*—Information technology is treated as just a tool for support of execution, not an integral part of the business operation. Viewing information technology as a tool can result in the technology-without-a-purpose or technology-for-technology's-sake syndrome. With this perspective, user groups often acquire technology in a piecemeal fashion to satisfy immediate automation requirements.

- *Confused system selection environment*—This can be traced directly to the lack of a process orientation in the distribution environment and a lack of actionable goals set by management. Secondary problems occur when the information system functions and scope are not properly understood either by the project team or by management, and the implications of change are not clearly comprehended and communicated to all those affected by it. The management of this risk revolves around the training and orientation provided to the team at the start of the effort.

- *Localized IT planning effort*—The process is functional in scope rather than part of an enterprisewide effort. A significant danger to the process and the competitiveness of the company is the assigning of planning and implementation responsibilities to a single department (a natural inclination of executive management is to assign responsibility to the IS or finance department). The lack (in many companies) of distribution operations and customer requirements and the lack of knowledge of the basic distribution business processes endanger the effort and place the company at risk. IS departments are often conceptually tied to a single platform and vendor. Furthermore, they might have a vested interest in maintaining IT development and selection in-house, while centralizing information under their control. These can be unsuccessful behaviors in today's competitive global market.

A significant risk to the vision of an IT-enabled future state of logistics is internal nonconformance. As stated earlier, IT must be a part of change and an integral part of the supply chain process, not a means merely to automate existing practices. Change can be a very traumatic experience in any enterprise and if every stakeholder is not convinced of the need to change, the system will lose its effectiveness. This lack of conviction can be traced to several causes, including a lack of ownership for cross-functional processes, process owners having no commitment to what they perceive as an MIS project, and the lack of a shared vision of a future distribution process.

INFORMATION TECHNOLOGY JUSTIFICATION FOR DISTRIBUTION—HISTORICAL SHORTFALL IN PROJECTED IT BENEFITS

The promised benefits of information technology have not materialized for many firms. Consequently, many executives are wary of projected IT benefits and the realization of potential promised them by their IS managers in terms of strategy and market success. Among the reasons for this mismatch of expectations are the technology justification/capital allocation process, which encourages overly optimistic benefits projections; a reliance on solely economic methods of evaluation; arbitrary hurdle rates encompassing all proposed projects; and the lack of importance given to customer satisfaction, time, and quality benefits. This reflects a highly focused financial view rather than an enterprisewide operations management perspective. An additional problem lies in the traditional roles for and attitudes about the IS function in the firm. These include the separation of MIS and users, the traditional centralization of mainframe computing, and the propensity of some companies to develop systems in-house. These past weaknesses are changing, allowing managers to implement the integrated distribution systems described above to provide the anticipated competitive benefits.

Justification

IT project justification is a vital element of the implementation and resource allocation process in the company. Traditional cost-based methods, such as IRR, NPV, and discounted payback period, are no longer sufficient or even appropriate in many cases. The justification techniques employed should range from economic to strategic analysis, depending on the scope, organizational impact, and level of IT and its integrative capabilities within the supply chain. Most important, the strategic nature of the IT project must be considered; it is difficult to quantify the dollar benefits of many large-scale distribution IT projects. Figure 7.12 provides the justification matrix utilized by one company for project prioritization. The prioritization parameters are based on *strategic urgency/benefit* (the strategic impacts of the project) and *improvement potential,* with a focus on time, response, cost, and quality. While the strategic aspect in this instance was essentially qualitative (rated on a fixed scale by executives following a discussion of industry and competitive trends and firm performance), the improvement potential was quantified using benchmarking techniques against "best in class." The selected projects included some for business process redesign as well as certain applications and connectivity development projects.

FIGURE 7–12
Information Technology Project Prioritization: Justification Matrix

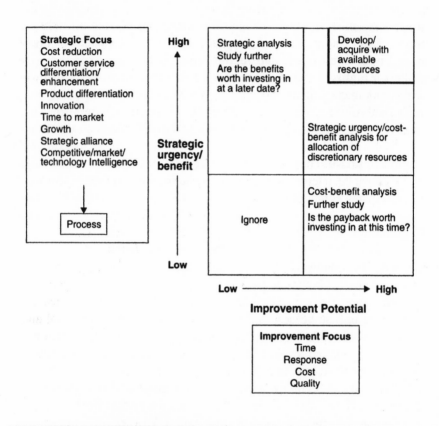

For such projects, much of the justification rests on confidence in the process redesign and strategic analysis processes. If the company is an industry follower in terms of technology, justification is fairly simple and can be based on documented case study benefits (through either benchmarking or secondary research) from the leaders. In this particular case, the company had lost some market advantage and competitive ground through excess conservatism and was striving to regain lost ground. For leaders, however, justification is more difficult, and its success rests largely on the rigor of the process redesign/IT planning processes and a good deal of faith in the people involved. One powerful motivator for investment in distribution systems is the presence of a *burning platform*—a change management term that refers to a crisis situation, usually in terms of customer dissatisfaction or competitor performance. In any event, too many companies place artificial and arbitrary hurdle rates on the justification process (often, a weighted average cost of capital plus some risk premium). These often pose serious problems. One large pharmaceutical company set an internal rate of return (IRR) hurdle of 20% and retained it for five years while its business, products, and competitive thrusts changed. This approach finally resulted in a major strategic information system, necessary to manage quality (a critical function in this industry), being rejected by senior management because the proponents could not come up with sufficient dollar benefits to justify the cost. This has led to a less-than-optimal situation—that of several small nonintegrated systems components being introduced in a piecemeal fashion to get under spending caps imposed by senior management. A cost-benefit analysis to justify information technology projects must consider all relevant costs—indirect, support, maintenance, training, and direct. Benefits must include cost savings and cost avoidance, ongoing operational and one-time (balance sheet) savings as well as revenue enhancement benefits. One large company quantified the following revenue enhancement benefits for a logistics system:

- Product availability.
- Improved service for after-sales support.
- Increased sales from ramp-up/delivery to distributors (another aspect of product availability).
- Faster response to orders for configured products (including OEM material).
- Cost recovery from warranty tracking of returned OEM products.

Finally, justification must account for the risk inherent in IT projects. Large IT projects are inherently risky in terms of time (system development and integration), quality (functioning as intended), implementation, and cost (overruns). These risks must be identified and planned for. An excellent justification process can be a competitive advantage in terms of systems deployment speed and effectiveness.

GLOBALIZATION AND DISTRIBUTION SYSTEMS— GLOBAL DISTRIBUTION APPLICATION TRENDS

Chapter 1 referred to the trends in globalization of markets and the management of global companies. These trends include increased geographical dispersion of the configuration/network and increased coordination of like activities along the supply chain. These are forcing manufacturers to acquire and develop new or greatly expanded applications to provide information and decision support to manage integrated distribution in this new competitive environment. Briefly, these applications include:

- *Global supply-demand planning* systems with global access.
- *Electronic commerce* (including EDI) to include other stakeholders in the firm—customers, transportation companies, contract warehouses, freight forwarders, distributors, and value-added resellers—as they move toward increased outsourcing.
- *Global resource balancing,* incorporating optimization modeling to manage assets (capital and inventory) along the supply chain.
- *Worldwide inventory and order status* (including lot status) and visibility.
- *Key indicator performance measurement and reporting* on a worldwide basis.
- *Financial reporting* commonality/consistency for management and investors.

Attempting to successfully manage integrated distribution in a global environment on a sustained basis in today's highly competitive environment without the functionality and integration provided by these applications is all but impossible. Several companies are attempting to develop these applications in-house, and, of these, a number are experiencing problems in time, cost, functionality, and user frustration (one large global components company is in its second major incarnation of the in-house development of a worldwide forecasting and planning system). Others are using a combination of in-house and off-the-shelf packaged software. Lessons from successful companies show that the latter approach so far has been more successful, generally, because software development is the core competency of most third-party developers, and most are very good at it. Furthermore, acquiring, modifying, and implementing such outsourced systems is often significantly faster than developing them in-house.

GLOBAL NETWORK IT OPERATIONS SUPPORTING INTEGRATED DISTRIBUTION

In response to globalization and competitive trends and the pressures imposed by these applications, many companies are reorganizing their IS functions and responsibilities and viewing the issues involved from a strategic IT perspective. They are moving away from the concept of user data access toward that of user self-sufficiency. The key strategic issue facing companies is that of centralization versus decentralization of information support. The new IS roles and responsibilities, which are emerging in several multinational companies, represent a balanced view of information support within the organization. Briefly, they are described below.

Functions and Functional Responsibilities

Increasingly, corporate IS is being called upon to play a facilitation and planning role. The essence of this role is integration. Global enterprises are realizing that the best IT applications acquisition decisions, applications usage, and maintenance are done at the local supply chain level. Hence, centralization is occurring in the area of ensuring that the enterprise can be fully information-integrated as well as in the management of core systems necessary to manage the enterprise from corporate. Included are basic functions such as core systems maintenance, but more important are the value-added roles of facilitation in strategic IT planning and justification, business process redesign, and systems integration. An equally important aspect of this role is standards-setting for the enterprise in terms of communications standards, protocols, and the integration requirements for the company. On the other hand, several functions that have long been the purview of a centralized IS group have been disaggregated and pushed to the local facilities/SBU level in the supply chain. These include the acquisition of key applications and their use, enhancement, and maintenance.

Key Applications and Responsibilities

Among the trends inherent in globalization are increased coordination of key activities and geographical dispersion of the logistics network, which pose unique challenges in applications selection, acquisition, development, and maintenance. Companies are responding by centralizing the core applications necessary for managing the global enterprise and decentralizing those applications necessary for management at a local supply chain level. For instance, these core applications can include global supply-demand planning and resource balancing, worldwide inventory/order status and visibility, common financial and key indicator measurement and reporting, and standards-setting. Key applications at the integrated distribution level include scheduling, decision-support, order configuration and fulfillment management, and expert systems applications. Centralization-decentralization here is typically not the issue; the issue is integration with production and customers and speed of development, implementation, and change.

CONCLUSION

Information technology for integrated distribution involves a great deal more than applications. It requires emphasis on integration with the rest of the enterprise and the supply chain, the role and function of the IS organization with respect to distribution, and full-featured applications systems that enable the distribution process. Distribution systems are critical in today's world of rapid and instant information sharing across the virtual supply chain. Their acquisition and implementation must include the efforts and support of all stakeholders including customers and suppliers.

LESSONS FOR MANAGERS

Given the pace of change in the marketplace and rapid advances in information technology, distribution managers must become aware of the fundamental capabilities of information technology in enabling their distribution processes. These capabilities include the effects on reducing geographical and proximity constraints, eliminating intermediate activities and non-value-added processes, facilitating rapid communication, scheduling complex activities (such as order turnaround in warehouses), and enabling portability (a typical method involves the use of hand-held and pen-based computers). It is important to note that this awareness does not have to involve detailed knowledge of the technologies themselves, just their capabilities. The distribution manager does not have to be an expert in information technology, but a knowledge, periodically refreshed, of its fundamental capabilities is essential to effective planning, design, and management of the integrated distribution process. Once generic capabilities are built into the process design, a cost-benefit analysis can ascertain the extent and types of technology that can implement the distribution process in a cost-effective manner.

Information technology has almost unlimited capabilities. The key for the distribution manager is in specifying and evaluating its cost-effective use and rapid implementation. To accomplish this, two factors are necessary. First, the realization that IT is an integral part of the distribution process and organization, not just an implementation tool, and second, a knowledge of the innovative ways that leading companies use IT as an enabler in their distribution process. This last can be acquired from benchmarking for best practices (not metrics) and collection of examples cited in the various distribution-related journals. This is a process that must be institutionalized (as it is, for example, in leading companies such as Xerox) within the supply chain function.

A final lesson to be learned is that information technology should be implemented in phases to allow benefits to be captured early and fund future implementations. This requires rapid acquisition and implementation and typically necessitates off-the-shelf packages and development outsourcing. The distribution manager must make the case convincingly to senior management that speed is paramount in such implementations. In instances where the technology is complex and its role is extensive within the supply chain, the role of the distribution manager must be to justify it based on strategic issues and long-term value to the corporation. This requires working with other functional managers within the supply chain and the enterprise. Localized IT decisions affect other functions—often in an adverse fashion. Supply chain and enterprisewide solutions (such as communications networks and information warehouse designs) require an integrated and long-term perspective. An excessively short-term orientation can render such investments impossible to justify and be detrimental to the future success of the company. If a distribution operation is allowed to become archaic because of a lack of long-term information technology investment, it is very difficult to change it into a competitive weapon without a great deal of organizational trauma.

CHAPTER 8

LEADING-EDGE ISSUES IN INTEGRATED DISTRIBUTION

This section discusses several of the leading-edge issues in integrated distribution. We have, earlier, discussed the role of integrated distribution within the logistics or supply chain. These distribution issues form an integral part of the overall new framework of logistics or supply chain management that will be presented at the end of this chapter. The concepts embodied in this new logistics framework are increasingly being incorporated into the visions of the future state of distribution for forward looking companies. As such, these issues increasingly form the areas of emphasis for companies seeking to obtain a sustainable competitive advantage in the logistics arena. Driven by competitive pressures, increasing customer expectations of product and service, and the realization that logistics is a key weapon on the new competitive battlefield of time and customer service, these excellent companies are envisioning and adopting the new frameworks and perspectives required of logistics management.

These leading-edge concepts essentially revolve around Stanley Davis's Future Perfect vision, which implies that the organization of the future will provide the customer with anything she wants at any time and in any place—the *mass customization* concept. While this vision is enterprisewide, it applies particularly to the execution of product-service-market strategy—in particular, the logistics supply chain and the role of integrated distribution within it.

The trend among leading-edge companies is toward a redefinition of the boundaries of the corporation, moving toward the virtual corporation that includes customers and suppliers. These alliances operate as a single process, sharing information, functional activities, expertise, and costs—resulting in a more powerful and responsive competitive entity.

Distribution is moving away from a purely warehousing and transportation emphasis to one that encompasses customers, suppliers, third-party alliances, and OEMs; in short, it is moving toward the virtual enterprise. The envisioning and enabling of leading-edge integrated distribution concepts involve a rethinking of the management of the supply chain as a whole, and their successful implementation necessitates a focus on managing the integrated supply chain rather than discrete functional pieces. These leading-edge distribution concepts, part of the new emerging logistics enterprise, include the management of integrated distribution to ensure consistent customer service across all dimensions and channels at:

- *Competitive total cost levels,* both total delivered cost (including billing and collections) and total acquisition cost from the customer's perspective.
- *Delivery* on-time every time for products and services to customer request date.
- *Time and response* to meet and exceed customer expectations for turnaround and service.
- *Quality* of billing, orders, packaging, and installation.
- *Convenience* of use, storage, and packaging to the customer.
- *The co-opting of the customer into the supply chain,* extending the supply chain into the customer's operation and tightly linking this extended supply chain to provide mutual cost and time benefits.

This implies new thinking on the traditional decision points regarding cost-service level trade-offs. It certainly involves the integration of design engineering, procurement, manufacturing, billing, and logistics to ensure a complete package for satisfying customers. This implies management and organizational integration with supply chain-wide performance measures based on market results. Products and packaging are being designed and tracked from the customer delivery, implementation, use, and service perspectives versus the traditional cost-driven approach that dictates maximization of cube and truckload lots. Total customer service, velocity, and time are the driving decision factors, with cost as a managed entity. Some leading-edge companies, for example, are specifying delivery to customer request (any time) and billing to customer specifications (any way). This requires distribution to maintain inventories and ensure rapid order turn-around to meet these customer demands, while upstream in the supply chain, it requires quick response to customer orders. Alternatively, inventory deployment to meet this goal may not be an issue if manufacturing responds rapidly to meet the order. Either way, the new environment demands the development of a high velocity, quick response supply chain with the ability to adapt and respond to a rapidly changing and inherently uncertain market and competitive environment.

Several macro trends in manufacturing and distribution have driven these competitive imperatives. Some of the primary ones and their implications for distribution management are discussed below. They include providing value-added services to the customer; increasing use of alliances and outsourcing as strategic options; direct customer involvement in product/service definition; advances in information and communications technologies; changes in thinking about organization structure, design, and employee empowerment; use of business process reengineering to improve distribution processes; globalization of the marketplace; and, finally, increasing deployment of expert systems as aids to decision making.

PROVIDING VALUE-ADDED SERVICES AS A COMPETITIVE LEVER AND TO INCREASE CUSTOMERS' SWITCHING COSTS

This dictates a new role for suppliers and distributors—that of component integrators and single point-of-contact vendors. Customers are reducing their supplier bases and, in the process, attempting to work with fewer overall suppliers. Some leading-edge distributors are consolidating their customers' purchases and providing services traditionally performed by customers—in effect, acting as procurement, manufacturing, and receiving/stocking departments for their customers. These value-added services are being actively promoted by some distributors and demanded by an increasingly large number of customers (for example, customers are examining their total acquisition costs to reduce their own purchasing, administration, incoming inspection, and inventory management costs) and revolve around the co-opting of customers into the value chain. Figure 8.1 illustrates the concept of co-opting customers into the value chain. These services include:

- *Consolidation, kitting, and shipment of procured parts from multiple sources in a just-in-time mode.* This enables customers to reduce the complexity of managing JIT delivery to production lines and the kitting functions traditionally performed by the stockroom. Some suppliers also stock the customer's warehouse (placing product and kits in the appropriate racks and entering the transactions into the customer's receiving systems), providing a single bill for services and goods. These reductions in in-house activities result in a streamlining of the procurement and warehouse functions, working with a single invoice instead of multiple invoices from multiple suppliers, and a reduction in personnel and other associated costs.

- *Value-added work (typically noncritical assembly, but, increasingly, operations that are critical to a company's competitive performance).* An increasingly large number of companies are outsourcing upstream to their suppliers those noncritical activities that do not make up their core competencies. Suppliers, on the other hand, are increasingly able to manage these activities as vehicles to sell greater volume and mix of components and material. For customers, the additional benefits lie in the lower cost and reduced complexity of management and scheduling.

- *Management of the customer's floor stock inventory.* Suppliers are extending their value chain onto the customer's production floor by managing floor stock inventory. In one case, the supplier's representative visits the shop floor every morning armed with the day's production requirements. Among the services (traditionally performed by the customer) provided are monitoring materials usage, computing daily materials requirements, and communicating immediately with the distribution center for replenishment. Delivery itself is rapid, enabled by advances in communications technologies.

- *Incoming inspection and testing.* The supplier's and distributor's roles are increasingly being expanded. They are becoming technical houses responsible for the production-ready quality of the material they supply and distribute. One method being used by several companies is for the distributor to take on the tasks of

FIGURE 8–1
Co-opting Customers into the Value Chain

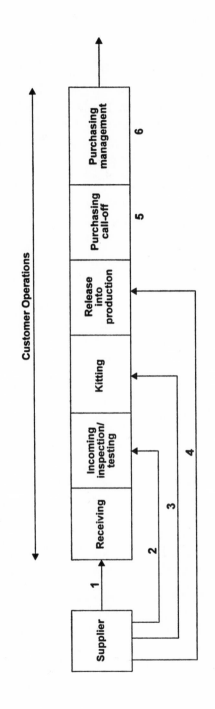

Stages of Assuming Customer Functions
Stage 1: Shipping to customer
Stage 2: Shipping straight to customer incoming inspection
Stage 3: Shipping Dock-T-Stock through quality/testing certification
Stage 4: Shipping direct to customer point-of-use/line
Stage 5: Delivering to replenishment levels at customer's stock
Stage 6: Procuring other components for customer—"one-stop shop"

Source: Ernst & Young Center for Information Technology & Strategy: All Rights Reserved.

incoming material inspection and testing (in one case, this extends to burn-in to test for component reliability). This reduces the customer's total incoming costs and provides higher margin services for managing these functions. The justification for such investments must incorporate long-term business survival and increased switching cost perspective (the use of short-term payback or hurdle methods of economic justification can often result in an outdated strategic response to changing market conditions).

Not all distributors are comfortable with these trends and customer demands. They must make the transition from traditional distribution (stocking and filling orders) to providing value-added customer service (performing customers' operations). However, several distributors, particularly in the electronics industry, are adopting such business practices as a means of attaining higher margins, selling more volume and mix, and increasing customer switching costs. In an industry where competitiveness has often revolved around price and availability, it marks a change to a new way of doing business, one of meeting a package of customers' needs and solving their business problems.

ALLIANCES AND PARTNERSHIPS

Strategic alliances and partnerships with key stakeholders—customers, suppliers, third parties with complementary products and services, carriers, warehousing, information technology developers, and integrators.

This trend emphasizes the increasing interdependence of the key stakeholders and moves them toward the virtual enterprise. While the electronics and high technology industries are certainly leading in the development of strategic alliances, this strategy is fast becoming prevalent in other industries as well. Among the strategic alliances that have significant impacts on the integrated distribution function and which must be managed effectively are:

- Delivery (both physical and electronic) of products to customers precisely when needed. This includes delivery to staging areas, end customer facilities, and customer production lines. In some companies, this has translated into building warehouses specifically for particular customers at their production locations. In an increasing number of cases, suppliers manage customers' interplant material movement and delivery in a just-in-time mode.

- Pick-up of suppliers' material at suppliers' facilities and return of packaging material. In some cases, this has necessitated specifically allocated trucks and warehouses for interaction with particular suppliers.

- Immediate response to customers' and suppliers' needs for delivery and pick-up of material. This often results in increasing localized distribution and information technology investments to maximize the potential and benefits of the strategic alliance.

- Working with alliance partners to define and develop business processes and information technologies and systems that integrate distribution and enable the distribution process. Third-party alliance partners are being involved to an unprecedented extent in the integration of the manufacturer's supply chain. Many manufacturers are linking into their customers' and suppliers' systems and processes in ways that enable the virtual enterprise. For example, it is now fairly common practice for firms to transmit orders through EDI directly into suppliers' order processing and, in some cases, materials planning and scheduling systems. In the process, some can monitor the status of the progress of their orders through the suppliers' value chains, provided they have inventory visibility through their supply chain. In some cases (Baxter Healthcare and Frito-Lay are examples), sales representatives manage their customers' inventory and transmit replenishment orders directly into the supply chain. An increasing number of alliance partners, particularly where third-party products are involved, are moving toward allocating inventory in their suppliers' inventory management systems, thereby further integrating the supply chain through the use of information technology. As a part of this trend, many alliance partners are now consulting one another for requirements and feedback regarding the design and development of information systems. A radical extension of this, highlighting the increasing interdependence in the industry, is demonstrated by companies that are actively involving their alliance partners in the redesign of their business processes. They solicit business requirements, product introduction plans, and channel management strategies as key inputs and test re-engineered processes explicitly for enablement of alliance partnerships.

OUTSOURCING

Outsourcing of traditional functions and value-added activities across the value chain.

Outsourcing is the strategic tool of the 90s. An increasingly large number of companies are outsourcing functions that have traditionally been performed in-house. Outsourcing can be particularly useful if, first, specialized skills that the organization does not wish to invest in or that lie outside its core competencies are required; second, the organization decides to focus on its core competencies in terms of management resources and investment; and, finally, the outside supplier or resource is able to deliver product and service quicker and more reliably at less cost or at consistently better quality than can be done internally. Outsourcing has touched virtually every aspect of the enterprise, including:

Supply—Manufacturers are reducing their levels of vertical integration, complexity of supply management, and supplier bases, resulting in a greater number of original equipment manufacturers and supply/distributor consolidators.

Manufacturing—An increasing number of companies are choosing to concentrate on key areas such as product development and manufacturing of proprietary technologies and are outsourcing other manufacturing activities to contract manufacturers. In the electronics industry, for example, this is a fairly common practice. Other companies, particularly in the consumer foods industry, are relying increasingly on co-packers. Outsourcing the manufacturing provides the advantages of flexibility and rapid change and eliminates the investment in, and management of, diverse manufacturing assets and operations. This can be particularly important strategically, allowing companies to assemble strong manufacturing capabilities.

Warehousing and distribution—Companies are increasingly outsourcing their traditional in-house distribution operations of warehousing and transportation to contract warehousing operators, full-service logistics carriers, and freight forwarders. Contract warehousing, for instance, provides shared risks of delivery, higher control and flexibility of operations, increased responsiveness to customer demands, and an often lower overall cost structure. Equally important, such contract arrangements create a business partnership in place of an arms-length relationship, with the entire distribution system working to provide customer service. An extension of this practice involves the outsourcing of the entire distribution function—from the production line door to the customer. Several companies now offer complete logistics services that include storage, order processing, and delivery to match customer requirements and manufacturer service level specifications.

Information systems—Information systems development outsourcing (not to be confused with the parallel trend of data center management and operation outsourcing) is increasingly employed to bring high quality information technology to users rapidly. Outsourcing systems development, particularly for new systems or the reengineering of existing systems, provides quick and immediate expertise in new technologies, rapid development, and an enterprise systems perspective. It can enable the alignment of IT strategy with corporate strategy and truly provide a competitive advantage.

Product engineering—Many companies currently outsource for the development of new products that lie outside their current lines and channels. They tend to outsource product development when greater flexibility is required and to cope quickly with changes in the business environment.

Process design—Companies have long outsourced for the design of manufacturing processes and equipment. This trend is increasing as process equipment and technology become more sophisticated and specialized.

After-sales service—While many companies have traditionally outsourced after-sales service (often to dealers and resellers) because of a lack of resources, they are now increasingly building alliances and outsourcing because of strategic direction. There are, as shown in Figure 8.2, several options for outsourcing and building alliances for after-sales service. These include, along a continuum of in-house to outsourcing, the following:

- *Field service maintenance*—In-house service planned and executed through company-owned facilities. The manufacturer assumes all responsibility for after-sales service and maintenance.
- *Customer-maintained*—Customers typically maintain the equipment and contract for its ongoing maintenance, if necessary, to third parties. The customer assumes the responsibility for the

equipment service and maintenance, procuring spares from the manufacturer if appropriate.

- *Third-party maintenance*—Pure outsourcing of all after-sales service to third parties. These third-party maintenance organizations typically are awarded contracts by the manufacturer. In some instances, the manufacturer imposes strict standards for quality and response; in others, however, the service is only as good as the third party that provides it.

- *Value-added reseller/dealer*—Increasingly, value-added dealers are providing service. Companies like Compaq Computer are training some dealers to provide service as a means of competing with companies like IBM that have large in-house service organizations.

- *Strategic service partners*—Companies are forging alliances to provide service for products, such as computers, that contain equipment from several different vendors.

In the past, companies tended to adopt a single option for their after-sales service function. Leading companies today, however, are outsourcing service on selected products based on margin (of service, components, and spares) and strategic considerations. For distribution, this implies the ability to respond quickly to needs for spare components and products from a variety of service providers. This response can be physical (delivery by truck or overnight shipment service) or electronic (delivery of software products) and increases the complexity of the network and its response capabilities. Some of the enabling technologies for managing the distribution for these new service outsourcing strategies are outlined in Figure 8.2. They include remote interactive diagnostics, networking, expert systems, and information systems for worldwide inventory, and spares planning visibility.

Outsourcing is giving rise to the *hollow corporation*, where the hollowness results not so much from chasing the lowest labor costs as from the following:

- A focus on core competencies and a realization that there are suppliers that can provide the rest quicker and at a far better price than can be done in-house.

- A need for flexibility in terms of change in manufacturing product

FIGURE 8–2
Field/After-Sales Service—Alliance/Outsourcing Options

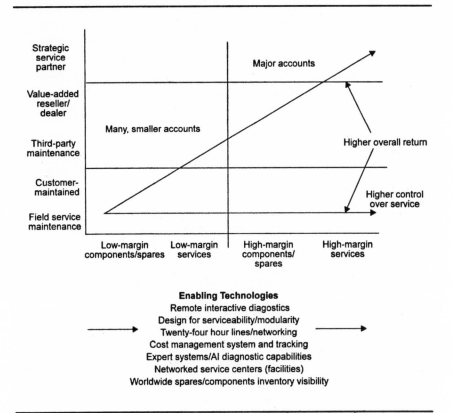

Source: Christopher Gopal and Gerry Cahill. *Logistics in Manufacturing.* Homewood, IL: Richard D. Irwin, Inc., 1992.

mix (requiring different modes and conditions for transportation, for example), delivery volume and region, seasonal, and storage requirements.

- Risk minimization in terms of investment in fleet mix, stock and personnel, warehouses and warehouse automation, information technology to manage distribution, and overhead costs in times of changing volumes and regional market demand. A particularly important example of risk is that incurred during production ramp-up for a new product.

- The strategic imperative of assuring excellent customer service at competitive cost structures. Outsourcing implies a partnership, and an increasing number of companies in all industries are discovering that this partnership can provide competitive customer service at better costs than can be achieved in-house. It allows companies to focus on their core competencies, whether they be logistics services, product design, or manufacturing.

CUSTOMER INVOLVEMENT

Direct customer involvement in the definition of the product and its packaging, specification of service requirements, and the pull-through/call-out of inventory.

Customers are becoming increasingly involved in the manufacturer's supply chain. In order to provide customer delight, companies are listening to *the voice of the customer*—inviting customers to specify their particular packaging needs as part of the product definition process. The implications for distribution are significant—the management, procurement, and stocking of a large variety of customer-specified packaging material and containers, often to go directly to customers' production lines. This customization of packaging requires flexibility in transportation and warehousing systems and the ability to handle endless variety. Customers are also specifying service requirements, transportation needs (frequency of delivery, lot sizes, location), and inventory call-off to match their production schedules. These trends alter the basic trade-offs between cost and customer service and call for the integration of total delivered cost into the decision-making process.

LINKS IN THE SUPPLY CHAIN

The advances and use of information and communications technologies to link key members of the supply chain and provide worldwide visibility, control, intelligence, and decision support.

Rapid advances in information and communications technologies have enabled the integration of the entire supply chain, linking customers, suppliers, channels, and third parties with the manufacturer. The key issues in successfully implementing this structure involve:

- Information technology (IT) strategic alignment with corporate strategy—ensuring that the vision and principles underlying the information technology strategic plan are consistent with those of the corporate strategic direction. Standards, particularly communications standards and protocols must be consistent with those employed by other stakeholders (customers, carriers, contract warehouses, distributors) in the supply chain.

- IT integration with business processes—making sure that IT enables the distribution process. Distribution process design must be information technology-enabled (not information technology-supported), and customers and suppliers must be involved during the process improvement and redesign.

- Information integration and sharing for the virtual factory—the integrated chain of suppliers, manufacturers, and distributors. Information integration allows the company to anticipate and be more responsive to the customer, rather than reacting to the competition. Information sharing is really a change management issue; few concepts are likely to generate more resistance than that of functional areas sharing information across the enterprise and with external stakeholders. Information is power, and sharing information reduces the hold of functional interests on the enterprise and enables true enterprisewide integration.

ORGANIZATION STRUCTURE

Changes in organization structure and design that provide single-point authority and responsibility for the entire supply chain.

This text deals with integrated distribution. As a concept, integrated distribution is no longer on the cutting edge of management thought and action; it has been absorbed into supply chain management, or logistics management. Integrated distribution, as defined for the purposes of this book, includes warehousing, transportation, outbound inventory deployment, and distribution information systems. This is, of course, a significant step beyond traditional distribution functions that included traffic and warehousing. The trend by many leading-edge companies toward overall supply chain management has significant implications for the distribution function. These include customer-oriented performance measures (versus more traditional measures of warehouse productivity and transportation cost as a percent of sales shipped). In addition, the trend creates the need for a new type of distribution manager—a multifunctional specialist (able to comprehend manufacturing, scheduling, and service in addition to warehouse and traffic management) with the ability to achieve multifunctional coordination, resolve conflict along the supply chain, and interact with customer manufacturing, procurement, and receiving personnel. Another key set of requirements is for information technology-literate personnel who can manage the introduction of new technologies for distribution as well as set the direction for MIS personnel in the organization. Finally, it demands the mindset that change is a constant feature of the distribution environment, and processes must be continuously improved and redesigned. This includes the ability to periodically evaluate operations and outsource when necessary.

This view of integrated distribution departs radically from the role of the traditional distribution organization and forms the distribution environment of leading-edge companies today and that of all successful enterprises in the very near future. This trend provides a powerful impetus to the customer-driven organization of the future when one considers the complementary move toward decision making.

DECISION MAKING

Empowerment at local levels, driving decisions down to the customer interface points.

This approach results in distribution decisions regarding delivery (frequency, lot size, etc.) being made at the local or regional level based on customer and profit requirements. The role of distribution and the supply chain is therefore changing to a pull-based response system, rather than a centrally planned, fully integrated function. This approach requires increased flexibility in terms of hard assets, inventory deployment, and transportation contracting. The supply chain, with distribution as an integrated end-point, thus becomes a supplier to the regional and local decision makers.

INTEGRATED BUSINESS PROCESSES

Business process redesign and the integration of process flow, information technology, facilities, and people with the customer.

An increasingly large number of companies are undertaking process reengineering efforts. It currently appears that the most intensive reengineering efforts are being directed at those multifunctional processes that touch the customer, most of which include integrated distribution. They are:

- *Order management*—This process includes order taking to fulfillment, which encompasses the integrated distribution process (see Chapter 3).

- *Sales cycle/order to collections*—The reengineering results from this process provide the requirements to integrated distribution in terms of time, delivery, and stocking. In terms of the future states envisioned by some leading companies, delivery to customer order must be executed within hours for some customers and products. This requires an enormously flexible distribution system—one that may include rolling inventory or highly distributed, high stocking levels of product.

- *Returns management/field service process*—As part of the entire package of customer satisfaction, this process is becoming increasingly important as a differentiating factor. Customer satisfaction on service criteria is, for example, being used as a competitive factor in the personal computer industry.

- *Supply-demand planning (or, as some companies term it, demand-supply planning)*—This includes the process from forecast generation through distribution planning and production planning, to procurement and third-party requirements planning. This planning cycle, which is shown in Figure 8.3, starts with the customer and moves back through the supply chain.

Unlike continuous process improvement, which seeks to improve existing processes incrementally, and traditional cost reduction efforts, which attempt to reduce localized costs, business process redesign is a *ground-up* redesign of the process, using the current process state only as a base line for measurement. It seeks to obtain orders of magnitude (5 to 15 times) improvements in total cost, time (cycle time and response time to

FIGURE 8–3
Demand-Supply Planning and Material Flow

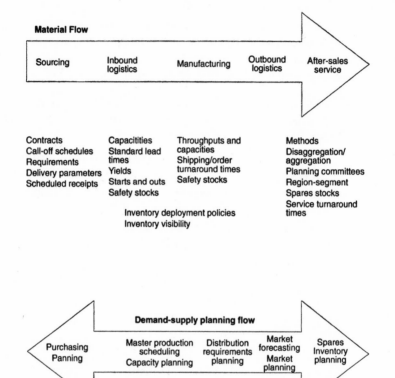

Source: Christopher Gopal and Gerry Cahill. *Logistics in Manufacturing.* Homewood, IL: Richard D. Irwin, Inc., 1992.

customer demands), and quality and typically involves the integrated redesign of process flows, technology, organization, and culture. Key requirements of the reengineering process include *benchmarking* for best practices (not metrics, as is commonly done) and *information technology enablement* of the process using both advanced and widely used existing technologies as guidelines for the new process. Following redesign and implementation, a continuous improvement program must be in place to improve the process until a performance plateau is reached or competitors leapfrog the process, when it then becomes imperative to redesign the process again. Given this continuum, it is vital that information systems development and implementation be rapid and that applications be treated from a life cycle perspective.

MARKETPLACE GLOBALIZATION

Effective management of distribution in the global arena as globalization increases in the marketplace.

Globalization has changed the way companies plan and operate. The requirements placed on integrated distribution are enormous and include:

- Extending the supply chain to include other countries. This requires a balance between planning for distribution globally and thinking and optimizing locally. Distribution in Europe, for example, requires local distribution centers, local management of transportation owing to differing routing through various countries, and adherence to local customs, export/import, and tariff regulations. Doing business in Japan, where overnight delivery is a fact of business, requiring local inventory to meet planned and ad hoc demand patterns, requires yet another mindset. Doing business in other parts of the Far East requires using local freight forwarders and extending planning lead times to account for increased transit times.

- Ability to ramp-up deliveries for simultaneous multicountry, multiproduct introductions, which often necessitate different packaging and labeling cube requirements.

- Familiarity with local tax and transfer price regulations (including U.S. regulations), which govern the value-added that can be produced in different countries.

- Interplant transfers of sem-finished material across national borders.
- Benchmarking best practices against the practices of foreign companies.
- Global resource balancing and organization structure.
- Accommodation to differing information technology standards and protocols (in EDI, for example). Linking systems and information around the globe poses enormous challenges to an information technology infrastructure.
- Monitoring and managing the changing logistics environment in many countries. A generalized trend is toward a reduction in nontariff barriers, administrative procedures, and restrictions in intercountry transportation for all modes, coupled with increasing concentration of distribution and freight forwarding companies. Such trends can, if managed correctly, translate into an increase in the speed and reliability of overseas carriers, a reduction in overall transportation costs, and an ability to ship smaller lots. The trends, in turn, are resulting in changing network structures for manufacturers. Several companies operating in Europe, for example, are consolidating their distribution centers and relocating them closer to major markets—in effect, treating Europe as a single geographical entity rather than a number of adjacent, regulation-specific countries. Integrated distribution operations for global manufacturers will now have to support rapidly changing marketing and manufacturing strategies, new product introductions (standard for some products and country-specific for others), and increased information linkage between manufacturing and distribution operations.

Europe—The Challenge

With the arrival of the Single European Market, U.S. manufacturers face significant opportunities and challenges; the differences in market preferences, transportation and warehouse infrastructure, and methods of distribution are wide across the continent. Logistics is a key to success in Europe, and the primary criterion for success will be the ability of manufacturers to adapt to rapid change and customize their networks to meet unique European requirements. Deregulation in transportation is giving rise to pan-European carriers with increasing consolidation in the industry—similar to the consolidation that has taken place in the U.S.

This is slowly eliminating levels of distribution in the supply chain. Currently, a manufacturer must deal with multiple vendors—in both transportation and warehousing, with resultant inefficiencies in costs and shipment consolidation. The new, highly competitive environment will result in trans-border order management, customer administration, invoicing, and inventory replenishment, at lower overall costs. This will be coupled with a continuing need to manage to different cultural and customer preferences. As in the U.S., network design will have to be customer-driven, with key distribution centers located at gateway entry points but with full-service regional locations to provide rapid and customized regional response. The hub-and-spoke configuration of major U.S. carriers like Federal Express is only beginning to emerge as a viable strategy (typically, a large number of shipments have been point-to-point). This current environment dictates multiple modes of transportation across regions. It must be borne in mind, however, that country-specific regulations will still exist and must be planned for in terms of paperwork, customs duty, and value-added regulations. Certainly, large European vendors have expertise in managing what is inherently a complex logistics environment, and outsourcing, as always, is a viable strategic alternative. Because pan-European full-service carriers are not as yet fully developed and this service is not readily available, it may make sense for the manufacturer to manage a number of vendors to provide market coverage and response.

The key to managing these trends is not so much structural as organizational—managing to multiple management cultures, European and global performance measurement, union rules, and the approach and concepts of quality in European operations. Working with these organizational issues in conjunction with developing and managing a logistics network to meet widely differing time-proximity and market-delivery preferences is the distribution challenge.

EXPERT SYSTEMS

The increasing deployment of expert systems in integrated distribution.

Advances in developing and deploying expert or knowledge-based systems have resulted in a tremendous upsurge in their application to distribution. Their ability to duplicate knowledge, learn by experience, process qualitative and incomplete information, and deal with uncertainty have made them ideal for applications within distribution—one of the more uncertain, variable-intensive decision areas in an enterprise. Many companies are seeking to extend the accumulated experience of tenured distribution managers with expert systems—in effect, enabling more people, through information technology, to make decisions that previously could be made only by the few experienced managers. These decisions involve ad hoc routing changes, multicarrier selection and contracting, and rapid stocking deployment to manage changing demand patterns. In general, the systems can make trade-off decisions based on intelligence within the system. Given this technology, managers can devote more time to real business needs—communicating and working with customers, third parties, carriers, and the rest of the enterprise. Among the applications of expert systems that are currently being explored or implemented in integrated distribution are:

- Inventory deployment—stocking locations, product mix, stocking levels, order turnaround parameters.
- Order taking and processing—ascertaining customers' needs, configuring products, assessing delivery schedules and availability, providing cost and delivery options to the customer.
- Carrier management and selection.
- Complex routing and routing changes based on ad hoc demand and product changes, including transportation mode and load planning.
- Cost-customer service level trade-offs based on changing market and cost parameters.

AN ENHANCED FRAMEWORK FOR BUSINESS LOGISTICS OPERATIONS

The changing industry dynamics and leading-edge concepts designed to meet them are transforming management roles and distribution imperatives, necessitating an enhanced framework for viewing and managing the business. This framework, which is illustrated in Figure 8.4, looks beyond current management emphases to envisioning the requirements of the coming competitive era. It encompasses:

- *Methods of cost management,* moving from a product costing to a total cost management perspective.

- *Business focus*, moving from product and process to a time-based, customer-oriented process focus.

- *Improvement methods* encompassing those providing significant improvements, such as business process redesign.

- *Organization structure and roles,* eliminating functional silos and utilizing multifunctional international teams.

- *Information technology* parameters, moving from value chain integration to stakeholder integration and global access with expert systems as the decision-support tools of necessity.

- *Employee motivation,* focusing on business performance rewards rather than functional targets.

The management perspective must shift from the traditional operational and functional mindset, past the current focus on the value chain, toward an enterprisewide focus on a virtual supply chain, which includes outsourcing where appropriate, strategic alliances with stakeholders, and planning for the global distribution system. In other words, the time horizon of strategy and execution must extend beyond strategic as is currently defined (three to five years) to the implementation of a vision of the future state.

KEY LEADING-EDGE DISTRIBUTION DESIGN CONCEPTS

Among the integrated distribution characteristics of this vision are several key design concepts (or *planks* of the vision) that leading-edge companies are using to redesign their distribution processes. They include:

- Total product configuration at point of sale/point of order, enabled by expert systems and high delivery flexibility, and including third-party material.

- The customer as an operational part of demand-supply planning, with EDI linkages into distribution and inventory databases and the ability to enter orders and allocate stock, even for third-party material.

- Packaging design specified by the customer, resulting in a large variety of packaging SKUs and lot sizes to be maintained and turned around by distribution.

FIGURE 8–4
Framework for Logistics

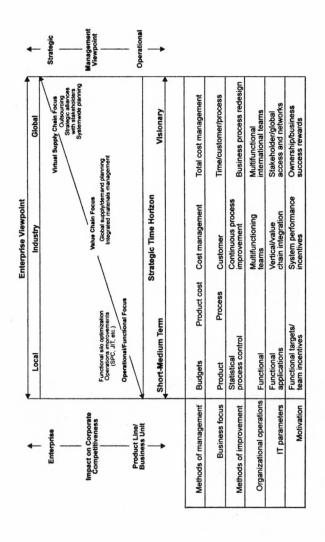

Source: Ernst & Young Center for Information Technology & Strategy: All Rights Reserved.

- Customers initiating planning and shipment of product through access and linkage with distribution systems.
- The *transparent corporation,* where customers have a single point of contact and do not see the various functional operations and third-party activities that meet their requirements.
- The hollow, outsourced corporation, where companies focus on their core competencies and outsource activities that require great flexibility at cost structures better than in-house operations. In some instances, this implies outsourcing the entire distribution operation.
- Information integration across the supply chain globally enabling all the other elements of this future distribution state.

These design concepts transcend the functional and enterprisewide perspectives to virtual supply chain integration and mandate a "break glass," or nontraditional, perspective on the roles of suppliers, customers, delivery response, and total cost. Integrated distribution is a key component of this virtual supply chain (where *virtual* refers to a highly integrated supply chain that is not necessarily vertically integrated but is, rather, a tight linking of the supply chains of customers, distributors, manufacturers, and suppliers), and distribution managers must change accordingly. It is clear that, in order to survive and compete effectively today, manufacturers must abandon the functional model of logistics management and operation and move toward an enterprise and virtual supply chain view. An increasingly large number of corporations in various industries are, indeed, adopting such a framework, using the leading-edge concepts described above as vehicles to arrive at this vision.

While this virtual supply chain forms a vision of the future state, manufacturers must integrate distribution with the rest of the company's operations. Chapter 9 describes the linkages among operations from a distribution perspective.

LESSONS FOR MANAGERS

This chapter has focused on providing new ideas for distribution managers based on those innovative methods and concepts used by leading-edge companies. If there is a key lesson in this chapter, it is that distribution managers must constantly seek innovative ways to cope with change in the marketplace. Successfully managing this involves the ability to view processes and issues from a multifunctional perspective. This book and the entire CIRM series provide this perspective. But this alone is not sufficient. Distribution managers must also study leading-edge companies (a study that must not be limited to companies within their industry) to identify how others are successfully addressing key competitive issues and rapid change. This should include innovative ways of using information technology in distribution, outsourcing activities that are not within the firm's core competencies, developing strategic alliances with customers and other suppliers, and reengineering the distribution process, if necessary. This chapter distills some of these companies' experiences—concepts that can be successfully implemented in a variety of forms in a manufacturing organization. It is, however, essential that managers institutionalize such benchmarking activities and analyze the results for applicability within their own organizations.

CHAPTER 9

INTERFUNCTIONAL AND CROSS-FUNCTIONAL LINKAGES

The thread running through this text has been the management of the supply chain through cross-functional management as the overall context for integrated distribution. We can, at this stage, identify the specific linkages of integrated distribution to the supply chain and the enterprise—in particular, those areas that comprise Integrated Resources Management. As with all major business processes, integrated distribution has important linkages and interdependencies with other functions. As one of the primary customer contact functions (the others being sales and, product development and design), its integration with the rest of the enterprise is crucial to the company's customer service and competitiveness. Figure 9.1 depicts these linkages and integration requirements in terms of planning and scheduling, response times, cycle times, quality, cost, and organization. Specifically, these linkages involve the following points.

MANUFACTURING PLANNING AND CONTROL

Distribution is responsible for the interplant transportation and warehousing of raw material, components, semifinished goods, work-in-process, and finished goods inventory. In addition, it must transport finished goods and spares to the various distribution centers (whether they be contract, company-owned, distributors, third parties, or customers). In order to execute this cross-functional process effectively, information integration in the business requirements planning system is essential. While the distribution

FIGURE 9–1   Integrated Distribution: Interfunctional and Cross-Functional Linkages

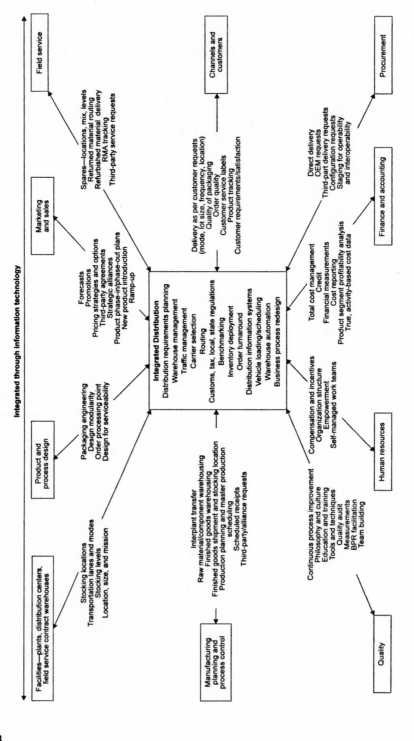

function provides information regarding regional sales expectations and usage (through the distribution requirements planning system) for incorporation into the forecast and the MRP II system, it must receive information regarding scheduled receipts, interplant ship schedules, master production schedule completions, and anticipated pipeline flows. These schedules must include shipments to and from third parties, OEMs, and alliance partners as well as direct shipments from suppliers. This information is essential for warehouse (internal and contract) space planning, public storage, warehouse personnel scheduling, vehicle scheduling, and specifying requirements for contract carriers. On a longer term basis, production plans play an important role in negotiations with contract carriers and warehouses and planning investments in space and equipment. The link must form a pull system with manufacturing, and manufacturing planning and control provides the vehicle to accomplish this customer-driven supply chain process. The distribution requirements and MRP II systems must be integrated into a single supply-demand management process if the company is to execute its marketing strategy successfully.

FACILITIES

Facilities typically account for a large portion of a manufacturing company's fixed costs. Decisions regarding lease, rent, or build can significantly affect financial results. Companies with far-flung distribution networks must, therefore, link facilities management closely with the operational decisions of the firm. The facilities to be planned for include those within the logistics network—plants, distribution centers, field service centers, and contract warehousing. Distribution must be kept informed of the changing product mix handled by various plants (including co-packers, contract manufacturing, and third parties), the different geographical segments targeted, and the capital allocation for upgrading existing facilities (racks and other storage equipment, automation, material handling) and acquiring new facilities. This information is essential for transportation planning for load, lanes, and modes of transport as well as inventory management flow and deployment at various stocking points.

Conversely, information regarding warehouse space requirements is needed from distribution to enable facilities planning and network configuration and rationalization (plant and distribution center location, size, product mix handled, and mission). These rationalization results are, in turn, used for distribution center consolidation (including satellite distribution centers, their lease or purchase) and transportation planning. Among these network decisions are those involving field service centers and the location of service facilities and spares stocking locations. Field service can be co-located in existing plants or warehouses or have separate facilities. This last option adds a degree of complexity to the issue of managing the movement (from and to customers) of returned material as well as the delivery and stocking of spares.

This is an iterative process that demands integration and information sharing between facilities management and integrated distribution.

PRODUCT AND PROCESS DESIGN

The interaction of product and process design and integrated distribution is often overlooked. This linkage, which is important to customer satisfaction, falls into four interrelated categories:

- *Packaging engineering*—This involves the inner and outer packaging of the product. The form of packaging will depend, ultimately, on marketing requirements (for example, "power" packaging for customer attraction, shelf space optimization, or customer convenience), customer requirements (semiconductors in cartridge-ready tubes and cartridges for easy use in the manufacturing process or specific lot quantities to facilitate customer kanban manufacturing requirements, for example), and transportation loading volume cost. A series of trade-offs involves customer service, shelf appeal and space, and distribution cost. Obviously, the denser the packaging in terms of quantity per master carton, the lower the distribution cost per truckload within weight requirements. On the other hand, customer-driven marketing decides the customer satisfaction and velocity of the product.

- *Design modularity*—The modularity of product design influences the storage and shipment of the product in several ways. For one, shipping semifinished product in modular form can be less expensive than shipping a complete product. The footprint and overall size of the product can affect storage space configurations and can result in some savings in terms of storage and material handling costs for more modular products and those designed with distribution as an input.

- *Order processing point*—The order processing point, or order penetration point (OPP) as it is more commonly known, is the point in the process chain at which a particular product is allocated to a particular customer. Product-process design is crucial here and must reflect the strategies of the company. The ultimate, configured product ("any way the customer wants it") may have its order processing point far upstream. This strategy, of course, depends on the company's ability to maintain short turnaround times on such configured, build-to-order products. While many companies today espouse this as a goal, it is not always an easy one to accomplish, requiring intensive product and process design, collaboration with equipment vendors and suppliers, and a complete reengineering of the manufacturing and ramp-up processes, with all their attendant cultural and human factors. On the other hand, it is always advantageous to move the order penetration point downstream (postponement). This has the advantage of time—increasing velocity through the system and enabling rapid system turnaround of orders—and can reduce overall cost through reduction in process complexity for most of the process. Many companies, for example, perform final assembly (where it is a fairly simple process and does not require complex testing) and packaging at the distribution center. Others pack and mark products at the DC, while still other companies use the DC for staging the product for final configuration (particularly where it requires multiple components from different plants and third parties) and box test. The costs associated with postponement include inventory carrying, warehousing, transportation, redundant processing (if the final operations are conducted in multiple locations), and personnel. These can be offset, of course, by significant advantages in time-based competition and overall processing costs.
- *Design for serviceability*—A vital element of the design for manufacturability spectrum, product design for serviceability, has significant impacts on the distribution network vis-a-vis field service center

locations and mission as well as warehouse spares requirements in terms of number of SKUs (modularity reduces the number of stockable items) and complexity of storage and replenishment. Designing for serviceability also influences the complexity of returned material. The goal is to have the smallest number of SKUs in the spares-returned material pipeline.

MARKETING AND SALES

Marketing and sales play significant roles in determining the ultimate success of distribution operations from the customer perspective. Marketing forecasts determine warehouse capacity and utilization plans and, as a prime driver of the manufacturing master production schedule, indirectly affect distribution planning. Nervous and/or grossly inaccurate forecasts cause as many problems in distribution as they do in manufacturing, leading to extra expediting activities and costs as well as bottlenecks and the end-of-the-month syndrome. Sales projections are aggregated on a regional basis for incorporation into distribution requirements planning—the front end of master production scheduling. Hence, the accuracy and stability of sales projections are of equal importance to distribution planning. Distribution effectiveness in meeting customer expectations of service also depends on timely information from marketing and sales regarding promotions (regional or national), which cause surges in demand; new product introduction plans, which require planning for transportation and storage; and product phase-in and phase-out plans, which determine the ability of the distribution function to adequately meet marketing strategies. Among the linkages with marketing and sales that can greatly increase the complexity of distribution are third-party agreements and strategic alliances that require:

- Pick-up and delivery at alliance partner and third-party facilities.
- Staging to ensure operability and interoperability.
- Coordination of simultaneous and/or agreed-upon delivery to customers.
- Returns management to noncompany facilities.
- Stocking and deployment of third-party product and spares.

• Inventory visibility into third-party systems.

Hence, the nature of the alliance must be examined to determine *true total* distribution costs to the company, and distribution must be involved in the alliance negotiations to set parameters, policies, and responsibility.

FIELD SERVICE

Field service forms an important part of the distribution equation. Response to customers and effectiveness in servicing breakdowns depend, to a significant extent, on forecasts of the need for spares, deployment of them in terms of mix and stocking levels, and replenishment policies. These are the responsibility of the integrated distribution function, and it is imperative that the link between field service and distribution be as tight as possible. Among the uncertainties are engineering changes, obsolete parts and supplies, and revision level management—issues that distribution must be aware of in planning for spares inventory deployment. In addition, distribution must be involved in the routing of returned material and the re-routing of repaired, serviced, and refurbished material. Several companies maintain service and refurbishment facilities at distribution centers, and inventory must be tracked, and often handled, separately from regular product shipment. An additional field service issue that enters into, and adds complexity to, distribution planning and execution is that of third-party service requirements. Third-party returns must be managed and routed to specific third-party facilities, replaced at the customer site, and returned to usable stock when repaired. This is particularly important if the third parties are OEMs and peripheral manufacturers. In the new environment of *one customer interface,* managing third-party service requirements becomes a vital customer satisfaction issue.

CHANNELS AND CUSTOMERS

These are obviously the prime interfaces of the integrated distribution function, and the requirements are set by the customers (channels such as retailers, value-added dealers, distributors, and wholesalers) and/or end customer users. Very often there are two simultaneous customers—the channel with its own delivery requirements in terms of frequency, delivery destinations, outer packaging requirements, lot sizes, and modes of transportation, and the end customer with his expectations of inner packaging, ease of conveyance, and returns processes. This last can be complex depending on the contract with the distributor. While most of the interaction falls into regular distribution practice, there are some issues that are often overlooked in planning for distribution and distribution information systems. These could involve materials returns and transport of repaired products to and from multiple locations, which could be even more complex if initial delivery were made to a central location while returns pick-ups and delivery were made to satellite centers. An additional issue involves the tracking (through either part identification or serial number tracking) of returned material, its repair, refurbishment and subsequent delivery to the customer. When the product has been replaced, it is often incumbent on the manufacturer to segregate refurbished material from regular inventory and treat it differently for resale purposes. These issues place large and differing burdens on distribution routing, warehouse stock location and management and, most important, the requirements of warehouse management, returns management, and tracking information systems.

While a significant number of customer satisfaction requirements are obtained from marketing and sales, the equally important customer expectations of service in delivery, response, order, and packaging quality are obtained through constant interaction by the integrated distribution management with customers. This interaction must be an explicit part of the responsibility of integrated distribution management.

PROCUREMENT

Despite the fact that procurement and distribution are at different ends of the supply chain, there are significant linkages that are important for customer service. These revolve mainly around the roles of third parties and original equipment manufacturers, particularly in pick-up (if the manufacturer is doing it) from the supplier and direct delivery from the vendor to the customer. This can occur with spares delivery, direct repaired product returns, or delivery independent of a completed order. In these instances, procurement and distribution must interact to ensure visibility and tracking of the shipment. This interaction becomes an even greater necessity when the third-party product is an integral part of the configured final product and must be staged for operability and interoperability before delivery to the customer site. This is a particularly difficult issue and is handled in several ways. Some companies, for example, stage at the distribution center. Others stage at the manufacturing warehouse, while still others stage at the customer site. This last can be risky, because it entails a degree of certainty that the configuration will work as planned. In any event, it requires excellent coordination between procurement, the third party, and distribution in terms of configuration requirements, delivery planning, and transportation scheduling.

FINANCE AND ACCOUNTING

The traditional role of finance and accounting has been one of reporting and financial services support to the distribution function. Included in these have been activities such as credit reporting, budgeting and financial planning, cost data collection, control and reporting, and cost measurement. The new paradigm of enterprisewide management defines yet another role for finance and accounting—that of decision support. A vital component in making the management decisions regarding customer service levels versus total cost trade-offs, warehouse and transportation productivity, inventory costs in deployment, and carrier evaluation involves the collection and aggregation of true cost data. An additional, nonroutine set of cost decision criteria includes costs and benefits for automation, technology, rationalization, and expansion investment decisions as well as outsourcing decisions involving make-versus-buy analysis. Total cost management involves ascertaining the true total cost of distribution activities to enable decisions on:

- Routing profitability.
- Total costs by carrier.
- Distribution costs by customer (warehousing, inventory carrying costs, and transportation).
- Cost breakdown by transportation mode.
- Costs of just-in-time delivery.
- Product-segment profitability analysis.
- Total inventory carrying costs to maintain set customer service levels.

- Network cost baseline for optimization modeling and inventory deployment decisions.
- Cost-benefit analysis for investment and outsourcing.

The two primary aspects of developing true cost information and profiles involve the approach to cost management and the information system to collect, stratify, and manage the information. Cost management should be based on activity-based costing principles, identifying key cost drivers and allocating indirect costs based on their impact, rather than the traditional method of allocating overhead based on direct labor. The information system must be designed to accommodate such costing principles and overhead treatment. The interaction between integrated distribution and finance and accounting must be a partnership rather than a hands-off reporting and budgeting relationship.

HUMAN RESOURCES

Human resources is a core function dealing with a vital asset (people). It forms one of the most basic relationships within the enterprise and, yet, its role is also changing dramatically. The traditional role of personnel management (counseling, policies, benefits, education and training, and compliance with government regulations, including OSHA and EEOC) is fast assuming a secondary position to the role of facilitating the new culture of competitiveness and total quality management. This culture includes the following attributes:

- Continuous process improvement.
- Internal and external customer-supplier orientation.
- Employee empowerment to push the decision-making power of the corporation to the customer contact point.
- Self-managed work groups that manage the business in a customer-oriented, lean manner, enabling rapid decisions and market response.
- Management of change in a dynamic environment where change is the only constant.

Human resources must facilitate the new paradigm of logistics management and the integrated distribution organization of the future. It must put in place the change management programs that can enable such dramatic changes. Among the most significant challenges facing human resources is the formation and nurturing of self-managed work teams in the warehouse and multifunctional teams for improving cross-functional performance and processes. This is a fairly complex undertaking that involves:

- Managing team compensation dynamics.
- Leveraging value in diversity.
- Implementing cascading performance measures that are consistent with corporate goals and customer requirements.
- Managing risk and encouraging prudent risk taking.
- Enabling individual and team empowerment that includes responsibility and authority, and, ultimately, the management and organization structure to facilitate company effectiveness.

Key issues are the management of expectations of both front-line employees and middle management, and compensation and incentives based on business performance. These issues are vital to the effectiveness of the distribution organization, and their successful resolution is incumbent upon input from, and decisions made within, distribution management.

QUALITY

The quality function has assumed increasing importance in many leading-edge companies today, with the emphasis on, and adoption of, the total quality management philosophy. Among the key business processes under scrutiny for improvement and redesign in today's environment is the order management process, of which integrated distribution is an important and integral part. The quality function can provide the conceptual infrastructure and the facilitation and training skills necessary to incorporate the continuous process improvement philosophy within the distribution function. This includes:

- Awareness of continuous process improvement philosophy and culture, including the competitive necessity for improving performance in distribution.
- Comprehensive education and training programs in the approach, tools, and techniques of continuous improvement. This includes

statistical methods to monitor, analyze, and improve distribution processes and performance as well as techniques to ascertain customer requirements.

• Programs within distribution to permit warehousing employees to visit customers and other companies to conduct benchmarking exercises for best practices and to collect information on customer requirements in terms of packaging, response, quality, and interface.

• Facilitating the development of quality improvement teams to improve the process and design and implementation of process and team-oriented performance measures. This includes team building exercises and training for multifunctional teams to improve the integration between functions such as manufacturing and distribution.

• Conducting quality audits (some companies base these on the Malcolm Baldrige National Quality Award criteria) to assess the effectiveness of continuous improvement within distribution. Care must be taken, however, to ensure that these audits do not degenerate into time-consuming and expensive exercises with little tangible follow-on. In some companies, such exercises have resulted in excessively large quality-related staffs and considerable employee cynicism regarding the total quality management implementation effort. The quality audit must be part of the improvement process, and it must have follow-on actions and measurable goals.

• A new role of the quality function, and one that is increasing in importance, is providing the expertise and facilitation necessary for the redesign of the integrated distribution process to provide improvements in cost, time, and quality. Business process redesign is an area about which the quality function in most organizations knows little.

In most firms today, the thrust of the business process reengineering effort, in terms of initiation, acquisition of skills, and methods, has been undertaken by the information systems function. This must be supported by the quality function if the company is to progress beyond incremental improvements. Unless a company's distribution operations are better than world class, there is quite probably a need to redesign the integrated distribution process from the ground up. Few companies are so good that they can afford not to undertake such an effort, particularly as competition continues to improve and customer expectations of service continue to increase. Given this environment, the quality function must acquire the skills and tools necessary to facilitate the redesign of the distribution process. These include:

- *Benchmarking for best practices,* not metrics. Benchmarking takes on a different twist in business process redesign. The thrust is to identify companies that are the best of the best with regard to certain aspects of the distribution process (for example, co-opting the customer into the value chain, rapid order processing and turnaround, consistent next day delivery, and using information technology in creative ways to enable the distribution process and its integration with the rest of the supply chain). The concept is to redesign integrated distribution so that the process is "beyond the best"; it should be the next benchmark for other companies. The intent here is not to focus on performance metrics, but the practices that make metrics good. Benchmarking for process redesign is more than measuring the gap between current performance and benchmark performance. It is identifying the best practices and the key design principles behind them in terms of process concepts, information technology enablement, organization, and culture.

- *Visioning and reengineering methods, processes, and tools,* such as facilitation, group creativity techniques, managing team dynamics, and structured team processes for reengineering complex and cross-functional processes.

- *Processes for ongoing technology enablement* to monitor new distribution-related technologies and the innovative uses of such technologies by other companies.

The role of the quality function is changing, from one of inspection and after-the-fact analysis to one of proactive management of process improvement and the quality of the process. This requires skills of expert facilitation and process experience as well as in-depth knowledge of the various tools and techniques for ensuring process quality. In several companies, the quality role has shifted to the process owners, such as distribution, while the quality function is retained as a central training and facilitation unit. These changing roles require a re-examination of the relationship of quality to the functions in the organization, with quality being incorporated into the operational fabric and quality departments coordinating resources and supporting field efforts at improvement.

CONCLUSION

The key to effective management of the integrated distribution function lies in its interaction with the rest of the organization. This interaction is enabled in two ways:

- The forcing of interfunctional management of key business processes through organizational change, facilitation of cross-functional teams, and performance measures that drive organizational behavior. This has been the theme of this text, and leading-edge companies have adopted, or are in the process of adopting, such changes.
- Information technology strategy, planning, and rapid systems development that enables this enterprisewide integration. As Chapter 7 on information technology for integrated distribution emphasizes, IT is the glue that binds the virtual enterprise. Development of systems, shared libraries and databases, communication, and the adoption of new technologies must be executed to this objective. Users, both internal and external to the enterprise, must be involved, and it is imperative for integrated distribution that these information linkages extend to customers, third parties, channels, and the rest of the enterprise.

The linkages described above are crucial if distribution is to play its competitive role as the front line of the company. Integrated distribution must be integrated with the supply chain and the rest of the enterprise if the organization is to compete effectively on the bases of time, customer service, and cost.

BIBLIOGRAPHY

This section acknowledges those authors whose work is referenced in this text and whose concepts and intellectual capital are embodied in this book. In addition, it provides the basis for a Reference Library for those managers who wish to probe deeper into integrated distribution management.

Abernathy, William J., et al. *Industrial Renaissance.* New York: Basic Books, 1983.

Anderson, David L., and Robert Calabro. "Logistics Productivity through Strategic Alliances." *Council of Logistics Management Annual Meeting Proceedings, Vol I,* 1987, pp. 61–74.

Anderson, David L., et al. "Integrated Operations: Redefining the Corporation." *Council of Logistics Management Annual Conference Proceedings, Vol I,* 1989, pp. 229–252.

Arthur, Jerry G., et al. "Baxter/Trammell Crow Company: Value Managed Relationship." *Council of Logistics Management Annual Conference Proceedings, Vol II,* 1990, pp. 31–66

Aucamp, Donald C. "The Evaluation of Safety Stock." *Production and Inventory Management, Second Quarter,* 1986, pp. 127–132.

Balam, Brian. "European Partnerships." *Council of Logistics Management Annual Conference Proceedings, Vol II,* 1990, pp. 267–274

Beer, Michael, et al. "Why Change Management Programs Don't Produce Change." *Harvard Business Review,* Nov-Dec 1990, pp. 158–166.

Bender, Paul S., et al. "Practical Modeling for Resource Management." *Harvard Business Review* 59, no.2 (March-April 1981), pp. 163–173.

Bhote, Keki R. "Next Operation as Customer (NOAC): How to Improve Quality, Cost and Cycle Time in Service Operations." *AMA Memberships Publications Division,* 1991.

Bishop, Daryl. "Outsourcing Transportation and Traffic Management Services." *Council of Logistics Management Annual Conference Proceedings, Vol II,* 1989, pp. 207–211.

Bishop, Thomas, and Seven H. Wunning. "Third Party Logistics: A Competitive Advantage." *Council of Logistics Management Annual Conference Proceedings, Vol II,* 1988, pp. 1–13.

Blackburn, Joseph D. *Time-Based Competition*. Homewood, IL: Richard D. Irwin, 1991.

Blanding, Warren, "Customer Service Logistics." *Council of Logistics Management Annual Meeting Proceedings, Vol I*, 1986, pp. 361–375.

Bowersox, Donald J., et al. "Logistics Strategy and Structure: Strategic Linkage." *Council of Logistics Management Annual Conference Proceedings, Vol I*, 1990, pp. 53–64.

———. "Integrated Logistics: A Competitive Weapon. A Study of Organization and Strategy Practices." *Council of Logistics Management Annual Meeting Proceedings, Vol I*, 1987, pp. 1–14.

Braithwaite, Alan. "Achieving Outstanding Logistics Performance in Europe—Post 1992." *Council of Logistics Management Annual Meeting Proceedings, Vol I*, 1991, pp. 257–292.

Buckner, Dennis, et al. "Third-Party Logistics: Key to Survival." *Council of Logistics Management Annual Conference Proceedings, Vol II*, 1989, pp. 341–351.

Busher, John R., and Gene R. Tyndall. "Logistics Excellence." *Management Accounting*, August 1987, pp. 32–39.

Byrne, Stephen. "European Partnerships." *Council of Logistics Management Annual Conference Proceedings, Vol II*, 1990, pp. 285–301.

Champa, Domenic J., and Gary T. Long. "The Supply Chain Perspective: The Customer Service Mix." *Council of Logistics Management Annual Conference Proceedings, Vol II*, 1989, pp. 149–155.

Christopher, Martin. "Assessing the Costs of Logistics Service." *Council of Logistics Management Annual Meeting Proceedings, Vol I*, 1987, pp. 195–204.

———. "Customer Service Strategies for International Markets." *Council of Logistics Management Annual Conference Proceedings, Vol I*, 1989, pp. 325–335.

Class, David J., and Craig K. Thompson. "Managing the Logistics Infrastructure." *Council of Logistics Management Annual Conference Proceedings, Vol II*, 1990, pp. 31–44.

Clayton, Brian R., et al. "International Transactions...An Integrated Systems Approach." *Council of Logistics Management Annual Conference Proceedings, Vol I*, 1988, pp. 133–160.

Close, Steve M., et al. "Knowledge-Based Systems: Achieving the Potential in Logistics." *Council of Logistics Management Annual Conference Proceedings, Vol II*, 1988, pp. 85–111.

Cooper, Martha C., et al, "Logistics as an Element of Marketing Strategy both Inside and Outside the Firm." *Council of Logistics Management Annual Conference Proceedings, Vol I*, 1988, pp. 53–71.

"Corporate Profitability and Logistics: Innovative Guidelines for Executives." Prepared by Ernst & Whinney for the Council of Logistics Management and The National Association of Accountants, 1987.

Coyle, John J., and Joseph C. Andraski. "Managing Channel Relationships." *Council of Logistics Management Annual Conference Proceedings, Vol I,* 1990, pp. 244–258.

"Customer Service: A Management Perspective." Prepared by the Ohio State University for the Council of Logistics Management, 1988.

Cypress, Harold L., "Exploiting the Age of Seamless Distribution." *Global Trade Magazine,* 1989.

Davenport, Thomas H. "The Impact of IT on Future Business Processes." *Executive Report: CASE, No. 1,* Winter 1991.

Davis, Stanley M. "Future Perfect." Reading, MA: Addison-Wesley Publishing, 1987.

Emmelhainz, Margaret A. "UCS/EDI: The Impact." *Council of Logistics Management Annual Meeting Proceedings, Vol I,* 1987, pp. 301–307.

Fischel, Dennis, and Ronald S. Potter. "Opportunities in Third Party Logistics." *Council of Logistics Management Annual Conference Proceedings, Vol I,* 1990, pp. 259–276.

Fox, Mary Lou. "Closing the Loop with DRP II." *P&IM Review with APICS News,* May 1987, pp. 39–41.

Garvin, David A. "What does 'Product Quality' Really Mean?" *Sloan Management Review,* Fall 1984, pp. 25–43.

Gopal, Christopher, and Cahill, Gerry, *Logistics in Manufacturing.* Homewood, IL: Richard D. Irwin, 1992.

Gopal, Christopher. "Developing Logistics Strategies for Competitive Advantage." *American Production & Inventory Control Society, 31st International Conference Proceedings,* 1988, pp. 370–372.

————. "Manufacturing Logistics Systems for Competitive Global Manufacturing." *Information Strategy: The Executive's Journal,* Fall 1986.

————. "Technology Justification: Obtaining Resources for CIM Acquisition and Implementation." *Pharmaceutical Technology,* April 1989.

Gunn, Thomas G , *Manufacturing for Competitive Advantage: Becoming a World Class Manufacturer.* New York: Ballinger, 1987.

————. *21st Century Manufacturing: Creating Winning Business Performance.* New York: Harper Collins, 1992.

Harris, Diana B. "Logistics Partnerships: Opportunities and Risks." *Council of Logistics Management Annual Conference Proceedings, Vol I,* 1990, pp. 213–224.

Hart, Christopher W.L., James L, Heskett, and W. Earl Sasser Jr. "The Profitable Art of Service Recovery." *Harvard Business Review,* July-August 1990, pp. 148–156.

Hayes, Robert H., and Steven C. Wheelwright. *Restoring Our Competitive Edge: Competing Through Manufacturing.* New York: John Wiley & Sons, 1984.

Hayes, Robert, Steve Wheelwright, and Kim Clark. *Dynamic Manufacturing*. New York: The Free Press, 1988.

Helferich, Omar K., et al, "Application of Artificial Intelligence—Expert System to Logistics." *Council of Logistics Management Annual Meeting Proceedings, Vol I*, 1986, pp. 45–86.

Henderson, John C. and N. Venkatraman. "Understanding Strategic Alignment." *Business Quarterly* 55, no. 3 (Winter 1991), pp. 8–14.

Herron, David P. "Managing Physical Distribution for Profit." *Harvard Business Review*, May-June 1979, pp. 121–132.

Heskett, James L. "Leadership through Integration: The Special Challenge of Logistics Management." *Council of Logistics Management Annual Conference Proceedings, Vol I*, 1988, pp. 15–21.

Hoffman, Lowell M. "The First Strategy in Integrated Logistics: Management Development." *Council of Logistics Management Annual Conference Proceedings, Vol II*, 1989, pp. 385–393.

Holcomb, Mary C., et al. "Managing Logistics with a Quality Focus." *Council of Logistics Management Annual Conference Proceedings, Vol I*, 1990, pp. 161–170.

Johnston, Russell, and Paul R. Lawrence. "Beyond Vertical Integration—The Rise of Value-Added Partnership." *Harvard Business Review* 88, no. 4 (July-Aug 1988), pp. 94–101.

Kallock, Roger W. "The Challenge of Managing Logistics in a Global Environment." *Council of Logistics Management Annual Conference Proceedings, Vol I*, 1988, pp. 83–93.

Kallock, Roger W., and David G. Robinson. "Reengineering Business Logistics." *Council of Logistics Management Annual Conference Proceedings, Vol I*, 1990, pp. 171–186.

Lambert, Douglas M., and Jay. U. Sterling. "Developing a Strategic Logistics Plan." *Council of Logistics Management Annual Meeting Proceedings, Vol I*, 1986, pp. 313–322.

"Leading Edge Logistics: Competitive Positioning for the 1990s." Prepared by Michigan State University for the Council of Logistics Management. 1989.

Livingston, David B. "Logistics as a Competitive Weapon: The Total Cost Approach." *Council of Logistics Management Annual Conference Proceedings, Vol II*, 1988, pp. 15–45.

Livingston, David B., and Gregory Lane. "Integrating Customer Service into the Firm's Strategy: The Times They are a Changing." *Council of Logistics Management Annual Meeting Proceedings, Vol I*, 1987, pp. 15–31.

Lounsbury, Charles B. "Profit Through Transportation Partnerships." *Council of Logistics Management Annual Meeting Proceedings, Vol I*, 1987, pp. 105–116.

Macklin, Colin L. "Third Party Logistics in Europe." *Council of Logistics Management Annual Conference Proceedings, Vol I*, 1988, pp. 95–121.

Masters, James M. "Analysis of the Life-of-Type Buy Decision." *Journal of Business Logistics* 8, no. 2, 1987, pp. 40–56.

Miller, Martin. "Strategic Planning: Visions for the 90s." *Council of Logistics Management Annual Conference Proceedings, Vol II,* 1990, pp. 241–245.

———. "Strategic Planning: Where the Rocks Are." *Council of Logistics Management Annual Conference Proceedings, Vol II,* 1990, pp. 247–250.

Muller, E.J. "Pipeline to Profits." *Distribution,* Sept. 1990, pp. 32–40.

Mundy, Ray A., et al. "Innovations in Carrier Sourcing: Transportation Partnership." *Council of Logistics Management Annual Conference Proceedings, Vol II,* 1989, pp. 109–113.

Murray, Robert E., and Samuel D. Calaby. "Outsourcing, Networking and the Hollow Corporation." *Council of Logistics Management Annual Conference Proceedings, Vol I,* 1988, pp. 171–235.

Neuschel, Robert P. "The New Logistics Challenge—Excellence in Management." *Journal of Business Logistics* 8, no. 2, 1987, pp. 29–39.

Novack, Robert A. "Logistics Control: An Approach to Quality." *Journal of Business Logistics* 10, no. 2, 1989, pp. 24–43.

Novack, Robert A., and Stephen W. Simco. "The Industrial Procurement Process: A Supply Chain Perspective." *Journal of Business Logistics* 12, no. 1, 1991, pp. 145–167.

Novich, Neil S. "Developing Superior Service as a Competitive Tool." *Council of Logistics Management Annual Conference Proceedings, Vol II,* 1990, pp. 257–266.

O'Malley, William J. "Japanese Logistics Systems: 'No Time for Tea.'" *Council of Logistics Management Annual Conference Proceedings, Vol II,* 1990, pp. 275–283.

Ohmae, Kenichi. *The Mind of the Strategist.* New York: McGraw-Hill, 1982.

Ploos van Amstel, M.J. "Managing the Pipeline Effectively." *Journal of Business Logistics,* 11, no. 1, 1990, pp. 1–25.

Porter, Michael E. *Competition in Global Industries.* Cambridge: Harvard Business School Press, 1986.

———. *Competitive Strategy: Techniques for Analyzing Industries and Competitors.* New York: Free Press, 1980.

Powers, Richard F. "Optimization Models for Logistics Decisions." *Journal of Business Logistics* 10, no. 1, 1989, pp. 106–121.

Pyburn, Philip J. "Redefining the Role of Information Technology." *Business Quarterly,* 55, no. 3 (Winter 1991), pp. 25–30.

Rao, Kant, et al. "Corporate Framework for Developing and Analyzing Logistics Strategies." *Council of Logistics Management Annual Conference Proceedings, Vol I,* 1988, pp. 243–262.

Rauch, Thomas J., and James Rust. "The PC Model: A Strategic Planning Tool." *Council of Logistics Management Annual Meeting Proceedings, Vol I,* 1987, pp. 159–181.

Robeson, James F. "Logistics 1995." *Council of Logistics Management Annual Meeting Proceedings, Vol I,* 1987, pp. 381–388.

Robeson, James F., ed. *The Distribution Handbook.* New York: The Free Press, 1985.

Schmenner, Roger W. "The Merit of Making Things Fast." *Sloan Management Review,* Fall 1988, pp. 11–17.

Schneider, Lewis M. "New Era in Transportation Strategy." *Harvard Business Review,* March-April 1985, pp. 118–126.

Scott Morton, S. Michael, ed. *The Corporation of the 1990s: Information Technology and Organizational Transformation.* Oxford: Oxford University Press, 1991.

Sease, Gary J. "Innovative Use of Information Management Models in Distribution." *Council of Logistics Management Annual Meeting Proceedings, Vol I,* 1987, pp. 149–166.

Sharman, Graham. "The Rediscovery of Logistics." *Harvard Business Review,* Sept-Oct 1984, pp. 71–79.

Sheehan, Willam G. "Contract Warehousing: The Evolution of an Industry." *Journal of Business Logistics* 10, no. 1, 1989, pp. 31–49.

Stalk, George, Jr., and Thomas M. Hout. *Competing Against Time.* New York: The Free Press, 1990.

Stenger, Alan J., and Joseph L. Cavinato. "Adapting MRP to the Outbound Side—Distribution Requirements Planning." *Production and Inventory Management, Fourth Quarter,* 1986, pp. 1–13.

Stern, Louis W., and Frederick D. Sturdivant. "Customer-driven Distribution Systems." *Harvard Business Review,* July-August 1987, pp. 34–41

Stock, James R. and Douglas M. Lambert. *Strategic Logistics Management.* 2nd ed. Homewood IL: Richard D. Irwin, 1987.

Taylor, Charles A., et al. "Developing and Managing Distribution Partnerships." *Council of Logistics Management Annual Meeting Proceedings, Vol I,* 1987, pp. 93–104.

Tyndall, Gene R. "Logistics and Profitability: Are the Two in Conflict?" *Journal of Cost Management for the Manufacturing Industry* 1, no. 2, Summer 1987.

Tyndall, Gene R., and Seymour M. Zivan. "Corporate Profitability and Logistics: An Update on Logistics Excellence." *Council of Logistics Management Annual Conference Proceedings, Vol I,* 1989, pp. 283–306.

Tyndall, Gene R., et al. "Corporate Profitability and Logistics." *Council of Logistics Management Annual Meeting Proceedings, Vol I,* 1986, pp. 295–311.

Van der Hoop, J.H. "Geographic Perspectives of International Logistics: Europe." *Council of Logistics Management Annual Meeting Proceedings, Vol I,* 1987, pp. 245–254.

Watson, James F., and Herb Johnson. "The Value of Strategic Logistics Partnership." *Council of Logistics Management Annual Conference Proceedings, Vol II,* 1988, pp. 277–290.

Weidenbaum, Murray. "Filling in the Hollowed–Out Corporation: The Competitive Status of US Manufacturing." *Council of Logistics Management Annual Conference Proceedings, Vol I,* 1989, pp. 1–13.

Wheelwright, Steven C., and Robert H. Hayes. "Competing through Manufacturing." *Harvard Business Review,* Jan-Feb 1985, pp. 99–109.

Zinn, Walter, and Donald J. Bowersox. "Planning Physical Distribution with the Principle of Postponement." *Journal of Business Logistics 9,* no. 2, 1988, pp. 117–136.

INDEX

G

General Electric Corporation, 6, 9, 65
Georgia-Pacific, 11
Global distribution trends, 6, 86, 188–90, 209–11

H

Heuristic modeling, 169–71
Hollow corporation concept, 202, 215
Human resources
  availability, 91
  link to integrated distribution management, 226–27
Hurdle rates, 187

I

Information
  centralized versus decentralized, 189–90
  customer requirements, 111–13
  integration, 205
  network performance, 115–16
  product cost, 112
  product delivery, 113
  product demand, 128–29
  product ordering, 112
  product requirements, 112
  sales forecast, 113–15
Information sharing, 176, 205
Information systems development outsourcing, 201
Information technology, 90
  aligned with corporate strategy, 205
  applications integration, 173–77
  applications strategy, 151–54
  applications systems, 150–73
  benefits, 184–85
  business process integration, 145–50, 205
  globalization, 188–90
  implementation pitfalls, 183–84
  implementation success, 8, 179–83
  in-house versus turn-key, 178–79
  organization structure, 180–81
  planning, 177
  prioritization parameters, 185
  project justification, 185–88
  project plans, 182
  relationship to integrated manufacturing and distribution networks, 147
  strategy, 19, 42
  trends, 5–6, 17, 145
Information warehouses, 173
Innovation for customer satisfaction, 74
Installation services, 52
Integrated distribution management
  applications, 55
  competitive advantage through, 22–24

cross-functional linkages, 217–30
  design concepts, 213–15
  implementation planning, 42–43
  objectives, 14, 24, 194
  trends, 22–24
Integrated inventory strategy, 19, 36–41
Integrated manufacturing and distribution networks
  components, 66
  cost factors, 80–84
  cost information, 116–17
  cross-functional linkages, 217–30
  customer delivery facilities, 66, 70–72
  customer satisfaction responsibilities, 72–75
  cycle time, 75–78
  design factors, 84–94, 123–24
  distribution facilities, 66, 69–70
  environmental forces, 88–91
  integration factors, 67
  manufacturing facilities, 66, 68–69
  measurement data, 92
  mission, 72–73
  monitoring processes, 91
  performance levels, 78–80
  performance measurement, 115–16, 121–22, 139–42
  performance metrics, 139–42
  purpose, 65
  relationship to information technology, 147
  role, 63–65
  transition cycle, 84–92
  value-added steps, 65
Intel, 11
Internal orders management, 45, 58–60
Inventories
  as buffers, 99
  finished goods, 105
  simultaneous planning, 107
  work-in-process, 104–5
Inventory
  carrying costs, 124
  customer impact data, 102
  defined, 98
  flow of materials, 99–102
  holding costs, 117
  level monitoring, 130–31
  locations, 98, 101
  operations costs, 117
  scope, 101
  time dimension, 99
  value, 99
Inventory deployment strategy, 9
  balance in, 36
  customer segment mix, 38
  data, 21
  defined, 2
  operating values, 40
  optimum stocking, 40

About APICS

APICS, the educational society for resource management, offers the resources professionals need to succeed in the manufacturing community. With more than 35 years of experience, 70,000 members, and 260 local chapters, APICS is recognized worldwide for setting the standards for professional education. The society offers a full range of courses, conferences, education programs, certification processes, and materials developed under the direction of industry experts.

APICS offers everything members need to enhance their careers and increase their professional value. Benefits include:

- Two internationally recognized educational certification processes—Certified in Production and Inventory Management (CPIM) and Certified in Integrated Resource Management (CIRM), which provide immediate recognition in the field and enhance members' work-related knowledge and skills. The CPIM process focuses on depth of knowledge in the core areas of production and inventory management, while the CIRM process supplies a breadth of knowledge in 13 functional areas of the business enterprise.

- The APICS Educational Material Catalog—a handy collection of courses, proceedings, reprints, training materials, videos, software, and books written by industry experts ... many of which are available to members at substantial discounts.

- *APICS The Performance Advantage*—a monthly magazine that focuses on improving competitiveness, quality, and productivity.

- Specific industry groups (SIGs)—organizations that develop educational programs, offer accompanying materials, and provide valuable networking opportunities.

- A multitude of educational workshops, employee referral, insurance, a retirement plan, and more.

To join APICS, or for complete information on the many benefits and services of APICS membership, call 1-800-444-2742 or 703-237-8344. Use extension 297.

Other titles in the Business One Irwin/APICS
Library of Integrated Resource Management

INTEGRATED PRODUCTION AND INVENTORY MANAGEMENT
Revitalizing the Manufacturing Enterprise
Thomas E. Vollmann, William L. Berry, and D. Clay Whybark

Discover how to slash production and distribution costs by effectively monitoring inventory. *Integrated Production and Inventory Management* explains the inventory control processes that optimize customer service and improve purchasing forecasts and production schedules. (270 pages)
ISBN: 1-55623-604-2

PURCHASING
Continued Improvement through Integration
Joseph R. Carter

A complete integrative resource for purchasing goods and services in the U.S. and abroad! As free trading zones open up around the world, the possibilities for sourcing nationally and internationally expand with them. This guide will help you enrich the buyer-supplier relationship that can lead to higher quality products from suppliers and more lucrative contracts from buyers. (200 pages)
ISBN: 1-55623-535-6

MANAGING INFORMATION

How Information Systems Impact Organizational Strategy
Gordon B. David and Scott Hamilton

This thorough guide provides a detailed description of the underlying technologies associated with information systems, including the roles and capabilities of hardware, software, databases, and communication technology. You'll discover how to use information systems to enhance the performance of all key operations. (360 pages)
ISBN: 1-55623-768-5

MANAGING FOR QUALITY
Integrating Quality and Business Strategy
V. Daniel Hunt

Maintaining a standard of quality doesn't have to cost a lot, but neglecting this standard can cost your company plenty. Hunt, author of the best-selling *Quality in America,* provides another excellent guide for achieving your quality goals—and effectively managing quality costs. (360 pages)
ISBN 1-55623-544-5

FIELD SERVICE MANAGEMENT
An Integrated Approach to Increasing Customer Satisfaction
Arthur V. Hill

How do companies like 3M and Whirlpool consistently rate high with customers in areas of field service repair? Hill, an established researcher and consultant in service operations management, examines their tactics and offers practical strategies to manage field service for high-quality results. (270 pages)
ISBN: 1-55623-547-X

Available in fine bookstores and libraries everywhere.